The Mirror and the Garden

Evelyn J. Hinz has taught American literature at the University of Saskatchewan and has lectured on the work of Anaïs Nin at the University of Massachusetts, Clark University, and the University of Manitoba, where she is at present a Killam Post Doctoral Research Scholar. She has published numerous articles on American and British literature in leading journals in the United States and Canada and has just completed a book-length study of D. H. Lawrence.

THE *Mirror* AND THE *Garden*

Realism and Reality in the Writings of
Anaïs Nin

☆ ☆ ☆ ☆ ☆

EVELYN J. HINZ

A Harvest Book
Harcourt Brace Jovanovich, Inc.
New York

The material on *The Diary of Anaïs Nin,* Volume IV, is based upon an article by Evelyn J. Hinz published in *The Journal of the Otto Rank Association,* Vol. 7, No. 2 (December, 1972).

Excerpts from the four volumes of *The Diary of Anaïs Nin* are reprinted by permission of Harcourt Brace Jovanovich, Inc.; copyright © 1966, 1967, 1969, 1971, by Anaïs Nin. Excerpts from *The Novel of the Future,* by Anaïs Nin, are reprinted with permission of Macmillan Publishing Co., Inc.; copyright © 1968 by Anaïs Nin. Extracts from the following works by Anaïs Nin are by courtesy of Peter Owen London: *The Diary of Anaïs Nin* (Volumes I–IV), *The Four-Chambered Heart, Ladders to Fire, The Novel of the Future, Seduction of the Minotaur, A Spy in the House of Love, Under a Glass Bell.*

Library of Congress Cataloging in Publication Data

Hinz, Evelyn J
The mirror and the garden.

(A Harvest book, HB 259)
Bibliography: p.
1. Nin, Anaïs, date   I. Title.
[PS3527.I865Z7   1973]   813'.5'2   73-4979
ISBN 0-15-660500-7 (pbk.)

For Jantje:

With thee conversing, I forget all time. . . .

Contents

Acknowledgments

The debt I have accumulated over the past five years to a number of individuals and institutions is indeed great, and this acknowledgment can only hope to name a representative few. First, I must express my gratefulness to Professor John J. Teunissen who introduced me to Anaïs Nin and who, from first to last, has aided me immeasurably with his encouragement, advice, and relatively gentle but constant prodding. Second, to Professors Douglas R. Cherry, Howard German, D. Sydiaha, for their invaluable advice in my first-stage preparation of this study.

I am indebted to the University of Saskatchewan and to the Canada Council for their generous financial assistance, and to the University of Massachusetts for providing me with a most congenial academic environment in which to bring this study to its present stage of maturity.

Only the finished product can express adequately my thanks to Richard Centing, editor of the Nin newsletter, *Under the Sign of Pisces*, to Jodi Davis, my editor at Ohio State, and finally, to Mrs. Helen Lesieur for her aid in the preparation of the typescript.

There are many others, and certainly they will find themselves shadowed forth in the pages of this book.

The author and the publisher wish to thank Anaïs Nin for her gracious permission to quote from the pamphlets *Realism and Reality* and *On Writing*. We wish also to thank The Swallow Press, Chicago, for their generous permission to quote from the following works by Anaïs Nin: *Children of the Albatross*, copyright 1959; *Collages*, copyright 1964; *D. H. Lawrence: An Unprofessional Study*, copyright 1964; *House of Incest*, copyright 1958; *Ladders to Fire*, copyright 1959; *Seduction of the Minotaur*, copyright 1961; *A Spy in the House of Love*, copyright 1959; *The Four-Chambered Heart*, copyright 1959; *Under a Glass Bell*, copyright 1948; *Winter of Artifice*, copyright 1961. Excerpts from *The Novel of the Future* are reprinted with permission of The Macmillan Company, copyright by Anaïs Nin, 1968. The quotations from *The Diary of Anaïs Nin* 1931-1934, 1934-1939, 1939-1944 are reprinted by permission of Harcourt Brace Jovanovich, Inc.; copyright 1966, 1967, 1969, by Anaïs Nin.

EVELYN J. HINZ

Amherst, Massachusetts
1971

That a new edition of *The Mirror and the Garden* has been called for makes me feel humbly proud, for I realize it is the increasing recognition of Anaïs Nin which has occasioned this demand. If I cannot entertain the belief that my book had some small part in shaping that recognition, I can at least feel pride at having been a pioneer in discovering her literary merits.

EVELYN J. HINZ

Winnipeg, Manitoba
1973

Foreword

The Recognition of Anaïs Nin

It is appropriate that Evelyn J. Hinz's first book of criticism should be a study of Anaïs Nin, for much of Miss Hinz's previous criticism has dealt with D. H. Lawrence, a writer whom Anaïs Nin acknowledges as an influence and about whom she wrote her first book, *D. H. Lawrence: An Unprofessional Study*.

The founding of the newsletter devoted to Anaïs Nin at The Ohio State University Libraries, Winter 1970, led to a notice of the publication in *The D. H. Lawrence Review*, Summer 1970, where Evelyn J. Hinz became aware of our endeavor and subsequently sent us the manuscript of *The Mirror and the Garden*.

The only book-length study to precede *The Mirror and the Garden* is Oliver Evans' *Anaïs Nin* (1968), which focuses on Nin's fiction and has a chapter on the first two diaries; it purposely omits any discussion of Nin's Lawrence criticism. The third *Diary* and *The Novel of the Future* were both published after Evans' study was completed. *The Mirror and the Garden* is then the first analysis of Anaïs Nin's entire published work. A bibliography of works by Anaïs Nin, with a list of secondary sources, articles and reviews, is supplied by Professor Hinz at the end of this book, and it should prove an invaluable reference for all future Nin scholars.

Anaïs Nin is treated throughout this study as an American artist, which should establish her as one of the most distinguished emigrés to the United States. Anaïs Nin refers to herself as an international writer, but for the sake of literary classification, she must be considered an American. The distinction would not be necessary except for the fact that arbitrary interpretations of her literary nationality—although she writes in English and has become a naturalized citizen of the United States—has lead to her exclusion from journals and writers' series with a national bias. (William York Tindall has indicated that Anaïs Nin had to be excluded from the *Columbia Essays on Modern Writers* because she was no longer a foreigner, while a recent anthology wrongly identified her as a French writer.) Actually, Nin should be considered a candidate for a series such as the University of Minnesota pamphlets on American writers.

The Americanization of Anaïs Nin does not mean to deny her deep roots in French culture. The first survey of her work appeared in Paris in 1964 as a chapter in a work by Pierre Brodin. Recognition of her work has been increasing rapidly in her native country, and she has been readopted by the French. A distinctively French honor has been bestowed on her by the recent formation in Paris of *Les Amis de Anaïs Nin*. Various homages and critical works are also in preparation. Herbert R. Lottman in "The European Scene" (*Publishers Weekly*, January 18, 1971) reported that the *Diary* was hailed by French critics as a major literary event. He wonders if "... her work will some day mean as much to her adopted country, the United States, with whose literary history she has been greatly involved."

The answer is yes. The recognition of Anaïs Nin in America has gathered momentum. There are courses on her work taught in universities; first editions of her books command high prices on the rare book market; her fan mail is enormous; for years she has lectured to students and professional organizations; dissertations are in progress; the majority of her work is in print, and translated abroad. In an interview published by Duane Schneider in 1970, Miss Nin said that she felt the reception of the published diaries was just. An audience for her work is established. The only element lacking is serious criticism; understanding.

The Mirror and the Garden now provides such a critique through objective insights into the subjective world of Anaïs Nin and the milieu of modern art and thought of which her work is a significant part.

RICHARD R. CENTING

Columbus, Ohio
1971

The Mirror and the Garden

Introduction

In one of her later publications, Anaïs Nin recalls a conversation with a professor who admitted to her that he had carried one of her books in his knapsack throughout the war, but had returned to America to write just another book on Henry James! "Why not living writers?" Nin had pointedly asked him.[1]

Although neither, perhaps, would satisfy the individualistic Anaïs Nin, there are two reasons why the critic feels more comfortable in the presence of the dead than of the living. In the first place, in attempting to define the work of a living writer one runs the risk of being premature.[2] A living writer is capable of outdating a study simply by producing or worse by changing. And unless he is purely professional, the critic like the artist is looking to the future as well as to the immediate present. Secondly, to write about a modern is to forfeit the support not of tradition but of time and its inexorable way of telling what will endure and wherein the ultimate value of a specific writer will reside. It is less because he mistrusts the writer than that he mistrusts himself that the critic pauses. To discover the classic in the contemporary is undoubtedly the aspiration of all who explore the work of living authors; but the desire, one knows, can cloud the judgment. It is therefore neither with ignorance nor arrogance that I undertake to accept Nin's challenge. Nor is it to announce that she is a neglected literary figure of the first order; rather my premise is simply that her art has not received the kind of recognition it genuinely deserves.

Because of the unsympathetic response her work initially occasioned, Anaïs Nin became for a long while the almost exclusive property of the group who, like her, were protesting the demands of the social realists. Then in the sixties, partly as a result of the efforts of her associates, partly as a result of the publicity her own lecture tours provided, her work became available to a larger audience. Unfortunately, and probably because of the lingering idea of the in-group, literary scholars have not touched her work and the task of interpretation has been left largely in the hands of "friends." This situation, understandably, can create only antagonism on the part of the outsiders, and could well return Nin to the small circle from which she has arisen.

---

[1] *The Novel of the Future*, p. 3. Complete bibliographical information concerning this and all of Nin's work is to be found in the bibliography which concludes this volume. A table of abbreviations is to be found at the beginning of that bibliography.

[2] I speak from experience, although a gratifying one. The bulk of this study was completed before the republication of her work indicated that she was about to become publicly recognized—and consequently before *The Novel of the Future* and the *Diaries* came into print. Fortunately they remarkably confirmed my interpretation of her theories and themes and encourage my present publication of it as an open-ended rather than as a tentative study.

1

In addition, at about the same time that she came into prominence, she was discovered by various recent liberation movements, who misinterpreting her independence and iconoclasm, have publicized her work as a contribution to their cause. Nin, the artist, was buried under the slogan of the woman and the rebel.

In general, then, Nin has received attention, but most of it personal or political; she is being read, but not for the right reasons or by enough of the right people. And what literary consideration she has received has been misdirected, owing in large part to that grand high priest of the *ex cathedra,* Henry Miller.

It was as the author of what Miller described as "a monumental confession which when given to the world will take its place beside the revelations of St. Augustine, Petronius, Proust and others,"[3] that Anaïs Nin became known to many readers. One must make allowances for Miller, of course; he was gargantuan in everything, including his financial debt to Nin, and her support and promotion of his own works. But it was not so much what Miller said about the *Diary* as that his words had the effect of directing all attention thence to the neglect and relegation to secondary place of her artistic and critical work. Thus numerous critics, following Miller and the American tradition of bigness, approach Nin's fiction essentially in terms of its relation to the multi-volumed *Diary.* Others scan the *Diary* for Nin's relation of the problems she encountered as a pioneer writer in America, then tell us to "read it and weep" at the plight of the woman writer, oblivious apparently, to the distinctly literary war in which she was engaged and the critical works wherein she outlines it, or that to buy one's own printing press is a highly aristocratic and slightly expensive gesture. Finally others, hearing her speak of her psychoanalytic experiences conclude that this "explains" her fiction, or noticing her iconoclastic attitude toward literary conventions assume that to approach her work one must be similarly avant-garde; neither considers the difference between her early and later writings, between the *Diary,* the fiction, and the criticism.

Thus it is the past and present critical situation with respect to Anaïs Nin that has motivated and consequently explains my approach. My purpose is to consider the work of Anaïs Nin from, as strictly as possible, a literary point of view, and to correct the current imbalance by focusing upon the fiction and criticism and to remove the lingering coterie connotations by demonstrating that one can approach her art with recognizable literary tools although not with nineteenth-century criteria. I have chosen a specific "theme" for two reasons. First, and here I admit my indebtedness fully, the Swallow Press publication of Nin's fiction, Gunther Stuhlmann's "Introductions" and editions of the *Diary,* Oliver Evans' pioneering study of Anaïs

---

[3] Henry Miller, "Un Etre Étoilique," in *The Cosmological Eye* (New Directions, 1939), p. 269.

Nin, and the founding of the Nin Newsletter, *Under the Sign of Pisces*—all these publications and each in its own way has made a study such as mine possible, and they will appreciate I am sure that when I take issue with one or the other it is in the interests of advancing not discrediting their work. By making the facts of her life known and her writing available they have provided a background without which my study would seem rootless and academic. A similar feeling of the need to see Nin in context explains why I have quoted abundantly from early critics and reviews. The second reason why I have shaped my book upon her theme of "realism and reality" is that such a procedure enables one to be restrictive without being limiting, a relative comprehensiveness so important when approaching poetic writers. I have chosen the title "The Mirror and the Garden" because it is poetic and consequently suggests the symbolic dimensions of all of Nin's writing as well as defining its poles.

To Nin's question of "Why not living writers?" the professor answered " 'Because we have no way of evaluating contemporary writers'." Like her I agree that this is more of an excuse than a reason. There are ways and consequently reasons why a study of Anaïs Nin is necessary and timely.

William Carlos Williams, an artist particularly interested in the "voice" of the American poet, suggests that there is an "authentic female approach to the arts," and that once this approach is finally recognized "Anaïs Nin may well be considered to have been one of the pioneers."[4] Most female artists, he suggests, are either on the defensive, and thus expend their energies in a negative combative way, or they are imitative, and thus attempt to reshape their intuitive perceptions in accordance with patterns and modes established by the essentially intellectual, rational male artist. Anaïs Nin belongs in neither of these categories; she is neither defeatist nor reactionary; she takes a positive attitude toward her opportunities and succeeds as a woman not because of nor despite her sex. Her writing—earthy and honest—proves that female artistry need not be feminine and precious; her writing—sensitive and intuitive—shows that intellectual analysis is not the only way to discover human motivation. At her best, as Williams observes, Nin "gives the impression of a woman for once sailing free in her own element."[5] While other women are concerned with merely demanding a voice, Nin is aware of the need to establish the quality of that voice. She wants woman to speak not as a mere equal or duplicate of man but as his complement. She wants a voice that is capable of expressing everything that a man can but always with distinctly female accents. In her writing she shows that this can be accomplished: she ranges from an earthy and unrelieved description of "the hoarse cries that issue from the delta in the last paroxysm of orgasm" to a

---

[4] William Carlos Williams, "Men . . . Have no Tenderness," *New Directions* (1942), p. 432.

[5] *Ibid.*, p. 343.

filigreed presentation of the "*mise en scène* for a great love." The authentic voice of woman is always honest and always in good taste, and it is this voice that the reader hears when he reads the novels of Anaïs Nin.

To the American critic in particular, the name of Anaïs Nin is important. There were two circles in the Paris of the '30's, "the lost generation" associated with the house of Stein, and the Villa Seurat circle including such artists and critics as Henry Miller, Lawrence Durrell, William Saroyan, Alfred Perlès, Hilaire Hiler and Abe Rattner. In this latter group Anaïs Nin was one of the key figures. She championed and supported, both financially and critically, the work of these men, corresponded with them, wrote prefaces to and reviews of their work. She assisted in the capacity of associate editor in the editing and issuing of the "house organ" of the group, *The Booster*, later renamed *Delta*. Frequently she appears in their writing as "the princess" or "cet être étoilique."

After the outbreak of World War II, Anaïs Nin returned to the United States and once more became the centre of an artistic circle. Her New York residence became the focal point for the following literary figures: Richard Wright, Truman Capote, Gore Vidal, Edgar Varèse, Marguerite Young, and Robert Duncan. Again she encouraged, criticized, and promoted the work of her artist acquaintances. Anyone interested in the work of the artists from either the Paris or the New York circle should be more than superficially aware of the name and writings of Anaïs Nin.

In the history of English fiction Nin is important as one of the early practitioners of the modern psychological novel. She began her explorations into the "Cities of the Interior" in the 1930's, shortly after James Joyce and Virginia Woolf had begun to make their inward excursions. Experienced in the methods of psychoanalysis, both as the analyzed and as the analyst, she is well equipped *materially* for the type of novel that she insists needs writing, the novel dealing with "the organization of the confusions within us." But she also has the necessary artistic equipment without which she could not have turned this material into literature: a talent for symbolism, a natural gift for rhythm, and an unwavering confidence in the truth of her perceptions. Vernon Young, commending her realization that the psychological is her "master subject" writes: "She has no equal in minute analysis, in conveying the nuances of expectation and withdrawal, the ambivalence of possession and surrender, the delicacies and gaucheries of contact."[6]

"The art of Anaïs Nin needs definition," wrote William Burford in one of the earliest critical articles on her work.[7] But it needs definition in two

---

[6] Vernon Young, "Five Novels, Three Sexes and Death," *Hudson Review*, I, no. 3, p. 427.

[7] William Burford, "The Art of Anaïs Nin," in *On Writing* (New York, 1947), p. 5. Oliver Evans similarly early recognized the need for a serious critical appraisal of Nin's work: "An understanding of Miss Nin's theory of fiction is, as I have suggested, indispensable for an appreciation of her work, and she has suffered considerable injustice from critics who were unaware of her intentions." See "Anaïs Nin and the Discovery of Inner Space," *Prairie Schooner*, XXXVI (1962), pp. 217-231.

directions. Because she is dealing explicitly with an area that is only implicit in the novel of the eighteenth and ninteenth centuries—the unconscious—she finds that she requires new techniques, which, as Mark Schorer suggests, are the only means that the artist has of "discovering, exploring, developing his subject, of conveying its meaning, and, finally, of evaluating it."[8] But although the techniques Nin uses take her out of the category of the conventional, they do not make her work esoteric, private, or coterie-oriented. In *The Novel of the Future* she compares her work to that of Djuna Barnes, John Hawkes, Marguerite Young and Nathanael West. The feelings that dominate her heroines and her direct and honest presentation of them may be suitably compared to Joyce's and Faulkner's portrayal of their females. Like Proust she allows emotion and memory to select and link the various episodes in her narratives, and like James she concentrates on what her heroines feel rather than do. Her ability to externalize subjective experience, to present a "drama of the unconscious" rather than merely a factual rendition of it makes one think of the inside-out novels of Kafka. It is as important to realize that she belongs to one tradition as that she departs from the other. Again, William Carlos Williams describes the Nin style as "spotted like a toad though it may be a lily's throat."[9] The work of Anaïs Nin is uneven, and for this reason a one-novel-acquaintance with her writing is not sufficient. In *House of Incest* she is lyrical beyond definition; in *Seduction of the Minotaur* she is frequently too objective. Both the "Djuna-Lillian" and "Stella" sections of *Ladders to Fire* are born of intense subjectivity; the former is transformed into a brilliant, complete creation, the latter in many ways resembles a still-birth. But when the novels are read in context and in succession the impression left on the reader is that here, as Rebecca West has said, "is real and unmistakable genius."[10]

Unlike Virginia Woolf, Anaïs Nin is not what one would describe as a sound critic, partly because of her awkward and vague use of critical terminology, partly because she uses psycho-literary terms without precisely defining them, but mainly because her best judgments are intuitive and, as such, very hard to express in "basic English." Furthermore, her quarrel with the realists, their views and techniques, is not an end in itself, a critical war, but an artist's war, an indication of a new trend in the matter and manner of creativity. Just as the early realists sought to overcome their eighteenth-century romantic and manners-minded fathers, so the twentieth century poetic and psychological novelists such as Nin struggle against the turn and first quarter of the century dispensers of panaceas and pessimism. Thus, while her theories may not be acceptable in a dictionary of critical termi-

[8] Mark Schorer, "Technique as Discovery," in *Forms of Modern Fiction,* edited by William Van O'Connor (Minneapolis, 1948), p. 9.

[9] Williams, p. 429.

[10] Quoted on the dust-jacket of *Spy.*

nology, in a history of the psychological novel they are definitely valuable. In this context it is not so much *what* she did as *when* she did it.

That the first book Nin published was an unprofessional study of D. H. Lawrence is not a coincidence. In theme, in style, in tone, the affinity between the English and the American artist are unmistakable. But Nin is far from being a mere "Lawrence redivivus." She recognizes his artistic failings —his solemn style and philosophical ponderousness—and largely avoids these errors in her own work. She recognizes the potential of the Lawrencean symbol, adopts and adapts it as her own controlling technique. She is in accord with Lawrence in his determination to do away with "dim half-lit truths" and "popular lies," but she is more subtle, more insinuating, perhaps more far-reaching than he was. Similarly, while the discoveries of psychoanalysis had a great bearing on her work, she uses this material in her own individual and poetic manner rather than in a clinical and impersonal way. Edmund Wilson sums up her debt to both influences in the following manner: "Though she owes something to Freud, as she does to Lawrence, she has worked out her own system of dynamics, and gives us a picture, quite different from that of any other writer."[11]

But it is at bottom because she is a highly perceptive, highly poetic artist that the work of Anaïs Nin deserves consideration and appreciation. Because her writing is in direct contrast to the themes and methods of the "so called realists" her struggle with them is the focus of this study. Today her objections to the philosophy and techniques of the Zola-Dreiser school are so echoed and accepted that the modern reader, unless he has read *The Novel of the Future,* may question the vehemence of her protest. But when Nin began writing, the novel of social criticism structured on the theory of biosocial determinism was considered by the majority of artists and critics to be the only novel worth reading and writing. Thus it took more than her own printing press and her own financial resources to publish her unsocial novels. It took personal conviction, courage, and determination. The following chapters may be considered as a tribute to both her artistry and integrity.

---

[11] Edmund Wilson, "Review of 'This Hunger'," *New Yorker* (November 10, 1945), p. 56.

I

* * * * *

The Mirror and the Garden

"DOES ANYONE KNOW WHO I AM?" (*House*, 20). The question appears so emphasized in Anaïs Nin's first work of fiction and reappears as a *leit-motif* in all the succeeding novels. It represents the central concern of both the author and her characters: the quest for and question of reality in a world in bondage to realism.

Unlike her precursors, Lawrence and Joyce, Anaïs Nin is not in any primary sense a philosopher or a theoretician, but like them she feels that "'. . . The absolute need which one has for some sort of satisfactory mental attitude toward oneself and things in general makes one try to abstract some definite conclusions from one's experiences . . .'" (*Lawrence*, 16). Experience to such writers refers to encounters not only in the everyday social world but also to confrontations in the world of literature. And the necessity for such a *personal* stock-taking arises from the modern artist's awareness that in the twentieth century science and psychology rather than religion and ethics provide the *données* upon which man relies. The old moral and aesthetic values, consequently, no longer directly correspond to one's practical experience, while the new cultural environment provides inadequate sanctions for either art or life.

Dorothy Van Ghent makes two observations concerning the writer in this milieu: first, the search for values becomes introspective, that is, a search for the self; second, the search for order becomes aesthetic, that is, a search for form.[1] The artist, his artifact, and his world become inextricably related; the respective questions, who am I? what is art? what is life? are answered simultaneously. In general, this situation leads to quarrels with traditional art forms and their supporting epistemologies. In the writing of Anaïs Nin the specific conflict is with the philosophy and literary trends associated with the general term realism. And in this context, the mirror is her symbol for the theories of her opponents, while the garden is symbolic of her own philosophical perspective and its related poetics. Critically, the conflict goes by the short title, "realism and reality."

In "a ritual to usher in a new life" Rango and Djuna, the lovers in *Four-Chambered Heart*, participate in a grand scale destruction of contemporary novels. As the books burn Djuna revolves the reasons for the destructive act:

All these novels so carefully concealing the truth about character, about the obscurities, the tangles, the mysteries. Words words words words and no

---

[1] See Dorothy Van Ghent, *The English Novel: Form and Function* (New York, 1961), pp. 245-246.

revelation of the pitfalls, the abysms in which human beings found themselves.

Let him burn them all; they deserved their fate. . . . Novels promising experience, and then remaining on the periphery, reporting only the semblance, the illusions, the costumes, and the falsities, opening no wells, preparing no one for the crises, the pitfalls, the wars, and the traps of human life. Teaching nothing, revealing nothing, cheating us of truth, of immediacy, of reality. (*Heart*, |48|)

Although Djuna does not name the offending writers, Nin not quite so cautious, elsewhere groups and pejoratively labels them the "so-called" realists.[2] In some ways, one wishes she had chosen a different term. James and Joyce, artists whom she admires, are usually designated realists; Lawrence, for whom she shows an early affinity, relies upon realistic techniques. Of course by questioning the accuracy of the label through the qualifying adjective, Nin does draw a distinction between the rightful and the usurping claimants. However, because of its slight clumsiness the qualifier must frequently be omitted. On the other hand, she just as frequently deliberately bares the term in order to contrast it with "reality," and consequently seems to contradict the initial qualification. Without condoning the lack of critical acumen, a lack not unusual in her critical writing, one can explain the reason for this choice of term. Realism is generally accepted as descriptive of both a literary technique and a philosophical position; it is because her thesis is that the two are inter-related, then, that she adopts the term. Virginia Woolf's "materialist," for example, would do for the philosophical aspect, perhaps, but not for the stylistic; "representationalism" might do for the literary technique but does not suggest a philosophical perspective.

By realism, then, Anaïs Nin refers to the documentary style of a Dreiser and to the philosophical naturalism of a Zola. It is, in short, what the general reader would consider the extreme in realistic practice and theory to which she is in basic opposition. And in this respect she is not alone. In "Notes on the Decline of Naturalism" Philip Rahv writes:

One might sum up the objections to it [naturalism] by simply saying that it is no longer possible to use this method without taking reality for granted. This means that it has lost the power to cope with the ever-growing element of the problematical in modern life, which is precisely the element that is magnetizing the imagination of the true artists of our epoch. Such artists are no longer content merely to question particular habits or situations or even institutions; it is reality itself which they bring into question.[3]

---

[2] *Realism and Reality*, p. 16. It should be made clear at this point that realism as it appears throughout this study denotes my understanding of Nin's definition of the term. It would be inconvenient to put it always in quotation marks, although these should be understood as implicit.

[3] Philip Rahv, "Notes on the Decline of Naturalism," in *Critiques and Essays on Modern Fiction*, edited by John W. Aldridge (New York, 1952), p. 423.

While Nin is not without critical support, then, it would be naive not to realize that there is a personal reason for her attack: as the inimitable Henry Miller suggests in "Of Art and the Future," "the artist is never defending art, but simply his own petty conception of art."[4]

Realism and Reality was written at least partially in self-defense, following unsympathetic criticism of her early fiction. To a certain extent, consequently, Nin's violent reaction against the realists is an inverse defense of her own highly subjective, highly poetic style. And because this is so, one can arrive at the basic principles of her theory of reality by an examination of her objections to the theory and style of her opponents.

Realism in the sense that Anaïs Nin finds it objectionable refers generally to the attitudes associated with the empirical mode of perception and specifically to the literary practice founded upon it, the novel of social criticism. In particular, literary realism for Nin refers to fiction which espouses objectivity on the part of the author, verisimilitude in terms of his technique, and social relevance with respect to theme. Based upon some form of determinism, it is concerned with socially representative figures and portrays them either as products or victims of environmental conditions. Denying transcendental reality, it stops at the visible world and thus its appropriate symbol is the Stendhalian mirror indiscriminately reflecting the blue sky and the mud puddle and blaming either the natural scene or the inspector of roads if the picture is shoddy.

Against such "endless book-keeping of existence" Nin, like one of her own characters, violently rebels: "Let me touch something warm. Save me from reflection" *(Bell, 42)*. One's first impression is that hers is the reaction of the typically aesthetic and poetic temperament which sneers contemptuously at the computer and the camera, and in part this is so. In her attempt to explain the genesis of a story, in "The Writer and the Symbols," she describes a situation in which she found "all the elements to compose a story. A volcano, Mayan ruins, Mayan costumes, mysteriously silent people. Yet none of these, compiled, tabulated, would create a story. They would only produce a travelogue."[5]

But her objection to fact and statistic goes deeper than a mere contempt for them as elements of an inferior form of art. As a result of "the fall," which to Nin as to many modern exegetes is a fall from a natural state to a civilized one, there is a discrepancy between appearance and reality. Facts and figures, be they ever so accurate statistically, may be utterly false as an index to the human condition. Since man, and modern man especially, has learned to prepare a face to meet the faces that he meets, appearance is often a disguise. "Men," she writes, "are their own impersonators," and thus "the so-called realists who believed they were copying natural man were only

    [4] Henry Miller, "Of Art and the Future," in *Sunday After the War* (New York, 1944), p. 159.

    [5] Nin, "The Writer and the Symbols," p. 33.

copying man's impersonations, the protective personnae [sic] by which he carefully concealed his deepest self."[6]

Her second objection, the objection to the subject matter of the realistic novel, stems directly from the first. If man is an actor then the type of action in which he is externally engaged is also a pretence. To Nin civilized society and the performance it requires are artificial in the pejorative sense of the word. Thus the sociological novel by definition evades rather than depicts man as he actually lives: "Most novels today are inadequate because they reflect *not our experience*, but people's fear of experience. They portray all the evasions."[7]

Clearly, then, the reason Nin attacks the realists is not that she is an aesthete arguing for the autonomy of art. On the contrary, unlike Virginia Woolf the reason that Nin is so concerned with the question of "the proper stuff of fiction" arises from her emphasis upon the educative power of the novel. Like Matthew Arnold she wants literature to assume the role that dogmatic religion is no longer capable of fulfilling, that of moral teacher and guide, though of course she argues for a humanistic definition of morality. According to Nin, it was because America lacked a literature of this quality that "The Lost Generation" came into being. "I believe that the experience of war might have been less disastrous to the mental and emotional life of young Americans if they had been prepared by an honest literature for all the deep primitive experience with birth, sex and death."[8]

But it is not only for war that literature must prepare the way. Daily life, especially modern life, also requires the vision of the artist. And since loss of identity seems to be the major characteristic of twentieth-century life, the artist's role is both to reveal the cause and to repair the damage by asserting the value of the personal and subjective. To do this Nin feels he must turn his focus from the realists' concern with external and social forces to the analysis of the individual and the synthesis of his inner or psychological motivations. In the same manner as Joyce proposed the development of the artist as a progression from the lyric-subjective to the dramatic-objective, Nin suggests that a similar progression is required by modern life. The error of the realists was their emphasis upon the objective to the neglect of the subjective and lyric. In *On Writing*, she explains the necessity of this inward turning: "While we refuse to organize the confusions within us we will never have an objective understanding of what is happening outside. We will not be able to relate to it, to choose sides, to evaluate historically and consequently we will be incapacitated for action."[9] By "outside" she refers

---

[6] *Ibid.*, p. 34.

[7] Nin, *On Writing*, p. 19.

[8] *Ibid.* It is interesting to notice that in this short analysis of American life and literature (written in 1947), Nin anticipates Leslie Fiedler's recent study, *Love and Death in the American Novel* (New York, 1960). That Nin receives no mention in Fiedler's extensive survey—either as novelist or critic—is consequently surprising, to say the least.

[9] *Ibid.*, p. 18.

not merely to social and political institutions but to all observable actions, stylized relationships, and mechanical modes of communication. By "within," she implies the spontaneous and instinctual level of response, "the irrational, the unconscious," which despite decades of suppression is still "the most powerful element in our character."[10]

Her third and final objection to the realists is to the philosophy of determinism and its tendency toward pessimism. The reason that she refuses to accept this outlook is not the Christian one (she views Christ as a personal projection); nor is it a result of naiveté (she welcomes the discoveries of modern science). This leaves only one other possibility and it is the right one: Anaïs Nin is to all intents and purposes a transcendentalist. As in the case of Lawrence, her emphasis on the unconscious often makes her appear more Freudian than Emersonian, but her insistence on "the emotional and spiritual content of every act and every object around us" clearly distinguishes her as in agreement with the American philosopher.[11] "Nature is the symbol of spirit,"[12] he writes; "It is the decoding of this content which should become for us a marvelous stimulant to our intelligence," she answers.[13]

Earlier we explained why despite the problems it involved Nin chose the term realism. We can similarly now explain why she uses the complex term reality to label her approach. Realism is cognatively related to reality, but according to Nin the former is the partial, the latter the comprehensive expression. Reality includes the realistic dimension but goes beyond it. Realism is an end in itself. Thus she does not deny the empirical world, but she considers it as sacramental, that is, an outward sign of an inward meaning. Not what the facts themselves demonstrate but what they portend is important. "The significance is the drama. The meaning is what illumines the facts, cooordinates them, incarnates them." It is by this process that she arrives at her definition of fiction: "The creation of a story is a quest for meaning."[14]

In view of her objections to the realists it should now be fairly obvious why Nin found their "mirror" to be not the conveyor of the real but "the perfect symbol of unreality and refraction."[15] The mirror reflects only the external, the mask, not the essential man. Also, the artist who records only what is reflected can only be a historian, never a prophet, for all he sees is what *has* happened, not what is happening or may happen. In one of her short stories the narrator explains this limitation: "To watch she must pause, and so what she caught was never the truth—the woman panting, dancing,

---

10 "The Writer and the Symbols," p. 38.
11 *Ibid.*, p. 35.
12 Ralph Waldo Emerson, *Selections from Ralph Waldo Emerson* (Boston, 1960), p. 31.
13 "The Writer and the Symbols," p. 35.
14 *Ibid.*, p. 33.
15 *On Writing*, p. 29.

weeping—it was only the woman who paused. The mirror was always one breath too late to catch the breathing" (*Bell,* 41). The role of the artist to Nin is to reveal the quintessential man (past, present, future, inner, and outer), not the two-dimensional scene (time and place). Reality expresses itself through the dynamism of the symbol; realism is necrophilic and seeks the image. Its world is not only static, a still life, but a type of death in life. "I saw in the mirror, not my death but the image of myself in the tomb. I was wearing a broach without stones, a crinoline with all its silk covering eaten away" (*Bell,* 42).

Because of the intense fusion of the questions concerning art and life in Nin's writing, a symbol representing the negative pole of art is applicable to the negative aspects of life as well. Thus the reflection in the mirror—two-dimensional, static and stylized—is used by Nin as indicative of the many varieties of artificial behavior and meaningless convention that have come to be associated with modern civilization. For example, in *Ladders to Fire,* Lillian, the aggressive woman at odds with a society that demands reticent femininity, finds that "the mirrors were scarred from the exigent way she extracted from them a satisfactory image of herself" (*Ladders,* 69).

Since conventions are taught and artificial behavior is learned, children are not concerned with mirrors. Thus the actress Stella, in "This Hunger," who has unsuccessfully tried to become her screen (mirror) image nostalgically reminisces: "she could not remember what she saw in the mirror as a child. Perhaps a child never looks at the mirror. Perhaps a child like a cat is so much inside of itself it does not see itself in the mirror. She sees a child. . . . The child is one. At one with himself. Never outside of himself" (*Ladders,* 38-39).

Finally, since neurosis is a pattern of unnatural behavior, a refracted rather than a natural reaction, the mirror is again an appropriate symbol. In *Seduction of the Minotaur,* Nin uses this symbol to underline the difference between the "native" and the "modern." The former sees with a "physical, naked vision"; the "white man" wears "dark glasses." In another of her short stories the prevailing tone and meaning is established by the simple title, "Under a Glass Bell."

The mirror as symbol in the Nin novels, then, has three referents: on the metaphysical level the empirical world, on the aesthetic level realism, and on the psychological level neurosis.

The garden had an air of nudity.

Djuna let her eyes melt into the garden. The garden had an air of nudity, of efflorescence, of abundance, of plenitude.

The salon was gilded, the people were costumed for false roles, the lights and the faces were attenuated, the gestures were starched—all but Lillian whose nature had not been stylized, compressed or gilded, and whose nature was warring with a piano.

Music did not open doors.

Nature flowered, caressed, spilled, relaxed, slept.

In the gilded frames, the ancestors were mummified forever, and descendants took the same poses. . . .

And then, as Djuna's eyes followed the path carpeted with detached leaves, her eyes encountered for the first time three full-length mirrors placed among the bushes and flowers as casually as in a boudoir. Three mirrors.

The eyes of the people inside could not bear the nudity of the garden, its exposure. The eyes of the people had needed the mirrors, delighted in the fragility of reflections. All the truth of the garden, the moisture, and the worms, the insects and the roots, the running sap and the rotting bark, had all to be reflected in the mirrors. *(Ladders, 139-140)*

Nin's choice of the garden as symbolic of all that is natural and positive in life and art is, of course, not original. As an archetype the garden recalls first, the place (wrong word) in which man and nature were in harmony, and second, the time (equally wrong word) when man was able to perceive meaning directly, before his vision was "darkened." Nin accepts these traditional implications and adapts them to each of the three levels on which her symbol operates.

As a symbol for reality, Nin's garden is the equivalent of Emerson's "nature," and the man who is able to read this symbolic text becomes, like Emerson's poet, "the transparent eyeball." Even if one did not have Henry Miller's suggestion that Nin was influenced by the American transcendentalist and his disciples, Thoreau and Whitman,[16] the following Emersonian lyric utterance from her first creative work would be sufficient evidence to support such a conclusion:

Significance stares at me from everywhere, like a gigantic underlying ghostliness. Significance emerges out of dank alleys and sombre faces, leans out of the windows of strange houses. I am constantly reconstructing a pattern of something forever lost and which I cannot forget. I catch the odors of the past on street corners and I am aware of the men who will be born tomorrow. Behind windows there are either enemies or worshippers. Never neutrality or passivity. Always intention and premeditation. Even stones have for me druidical expressions. *(House, 31-32)*

And just as Emerson's theory of nature led directly to his theory of the qualifications necessary for the poet, so Nin's theory of reality shapes her concept of the desired literature:" Modern art is a return of the symbol."[17] Since, as Coleridge has said, the symbol partakes of the reality which it renders intelligible, symbolic writing is a "return to the garden" in a literary sense.

Structurally, the garden refers to "organic" as opposed to mechanic form; stylistically it symbolizes naturalness as opposed to a classical or documentary style. Despite her emphasis on spontaneity, however, Nin is not a surrealist, nor a believer in automatic writing. She insists that the writer recognize and

---

16 Miller, *Letters to Anaïs Nin,* edited by Gunther Stuhlmann (New York, 1965), p. 49.
17 "The Writer and the Symbols," p. 35.

utilize the potential of the unconscious, but only as raw material to be fashioned:

> Some writers have brought the irrational streams into visibility but like reporters unable to extract either philosophical or psychological deductions from their findings, they emptied their vast nets filled with chaos and threw debris and absurd juxtapositions at our feet. This was what they found at the bottom of their unconscious. But few gave this a form, a meaning, sifting it and rearranging it with intelligence. They left it all for us to interpret. I am thinking now of many surrealist writers.[18]

In the original passage in which Nin first presented her symbols, the mirror was in the garden. The language of reality must be symbolic, that is it must be a *combination* of the visible and invisible. Abstractions, whether of the surrealistic or idealistic type omit this necessary foot-hold. Realism, on the other hand, never gets beyond the threshold. Reality, the garden, is a fusion of the two extremes.

Just as the mirror is the symbol of neurosis on the psychological level, so the garden is the symbol of psychic health. "Everything is alive or dead according to transcendental definitions of life or death" she writes in her unprofessional study of D. H. Lawrence (*Lawrence*, 17), and it is by this standard that she judges and sentences her characters. Stella, for example, in the novelette bearing her name, refuses to overcome her childish father fixation. Nin's assessment of such a neurosis is presented by an inversion of the garden symbolism: "People sent her enormous bouquets of rare flowers. Continued to send them. She signed the receipts, she even signed notes of thanks. Flowers for the dead, she murmured. With only a little wire and a round frame, they would do as well" (*Ladders*, 64).

The healthy psyche, on the other hand, is like the healthy plant, changing and adapting in an eternal metamorphosis, like the dancer in *House of Incest*: "And she danced; she danced with the rhythms of the earth's circles; she turned with the earth turning, like a disk, turning all faces to light and darkness evenly, dancing towards daylight" (*House*, 52).

The garden as symbol in the Nin novels, therefore, represents all that is positive, creative, and healthy. On the metaphysical level it refers to transcendental reality; on the aesthetic level it refers to a poetic style and organic form; and on the psychological level it refers to naturalness, spontaneity, and creativity.

Though one might find Nin's theory of "realism and reality" a bit confusing in places, and though at times it would be better if she were less poetic and more critical, there is no denying that her choice of symbols is apt and accurate for specific purposes. Her conversion of her opponents' vaunted symbol into a negative one is a neat turn of the screw; her adaptation of the garden as the symbol of her own concept of reality is an excellent demonstration of the way the individual talent utilizes the power of tradition.

---

[18] *Ibid.*, p. 39.

II

☆ ☆ ☆ ☆ ☆

A Word About Influences and Unprofessional Studies

" 'You and I,' " Nin quotes one of Lawrence's characters as saying, " 'let us begin at the beginning without jumping to conclusions.' And he begins the slow, tortuous journey: 'What are you? What am I? What is love? What is the centre of our life?' " "It is not," she explains, a matter of a "struggle" between the two characters "but one of revaluation."[1] The situation applies in an illustrative way to the following discussion of the work from which it is taken—*D. H. Lawrence: An Unprofessional Study* (Paris, 1932).

Because Anaïs Nin's first publication took the form of a "study" of Lawrence two assumptions have arisen concerning this work in particular and her art in general: first, that the Lawrence book is a piece of criticism and consequently to be apprehended in terms of its critical values; and second, that what resembles Lawrence's practice in her later fiction can be ascribed to his influence. Understandable as such assumptions are, and possibly even acceptable as they might be to the Lawrence scholar or the general historian of literature, in a study of Nin's art they must be questioned. For while the logic is sound the initial premise may be faulty, and as Nin herself expressed the problem, "The assumption of what is natural may rise out of a wrong premise" (34).

"Fiction such as Anaïs Nin's poses a peculiar problem for the literary critic," writes Oliver Evans in his early full-length study of her work, "for the critic is essentially a rational creature, and he must use the language of rational discourse," whereas he points out, Nin's appeal is essentially emotional. He resolves the problem by conceiving "the primary function of criticism to be illumination rather than judgment," and then concludes his analysis of the critical problem with the note: "Finally, because this [his] book was conceived as criticism rather than criticism of criticism, I have omitted any discussion of Anaïs Nin's first book, a critical appreciation of D.H. Lawrence."[2] With a similar conception of the methods and function

---

[1] Nin, *Lawrence*, p. 79. (Since this chapter is concerned exclusively with this work, the abbreviated title will be omitted from the reference and the identification will consist simply of the page number in parenthesis. Since the purpose of this chapter is to suggest that Nin's "study" is not the usual critical work, I will not be specifically concerned with suggesting the accuracy of her quotations or of their sources; in the interests of scholarship, however, I will indicate obvious errors and will indicate when she is quoting from Lawrence by using double and single quotation marks, as in the opening sentence.)

[2] Evans, *Anaïs Nin*, pp. xv-xvii.

of criticism others have attempted to explain the subtitle of the work, "An Unprofessional Study." To the reviewer of the 1962 reprint[3] as to Harry T. Moore in his introduction to the 1964 reprint, the subtitle is a reflection of the "modesty" of Miss Nin; to the former this modesty is appropriate, to the latter, unwarranted; but common to both, as to Evans, is the professional concept of criticism on the one hand, and the assumption that Nin's study is so orientated on the other. To the 1962 reviewer "unprofessional" is appropriate because the work does not measure up to "academic" standards, and Nin's use of the adjective indicates her awareness of her amateur performance; to Moore the adjective is unwarranted because the book does what criticism is supposed to do—provide an "explication of Lawrence"; indeed, to him it is "one of the most valuable books on Lawrence because of its discussion of the texture of his work";[4] while to Evans, Nin's study of Lawrence is comparable in principle to his own criticism of her work and consequently is out of place in his discussion of her creative writing.

With the definition of criticism that informs these observations one can only agree, of course. And so, in her own way, does Nin: "A critical faculty is a kind of lucidity which arrests impulses" (77). What requires questioning is the assumption that her "study" of Lawrence is to be considered as criticism of this variety, that the rationale of the work is an explication of Lawrence's art. Three reasons in particular urge such an enquiry. First, if one approaches the work as standard criticism, then one must honestly admit the justice of the caustic reviewer who observed that "its accuracy can best be exemplified by its three references to 'Studies in Classic American Literature.' They are, in order, 'Classical Studies in American Literature, Studies in American Classical Literature, and Studies in Classical American Literature.' "[5] But this is not to suggest that one must look for a different way of approaching the work in order to salvage it—Nin is good enough later to support an awkward beginning. Rather, it is because, justified as the condemnation is, when one examines Nin's "study" that condemnation seems irrelevant. This leads to the second reason. Despite Moore's claims for the work, Lawrence scholars have not found the book invaluable, to judge by the absence of allusion to it in studies of the last decade. This indifference could mean that critics have felt that the work has nothing important to say about Lawrence, but it could also mean that they have felt that Nin is not really concerned with Lawrence in the same way that they are, and that consequently it would be unwise positively or negatively to introduce her comments into their discussions.

Conjectural as these first two assumptions may be, however, the last is of a very different nature. It is Nin's "modesty," we have been told, that

[3] "Private View," *Times Literary Supplement*, XLI (March 16, 1962), p. 186.
[4] Harry T. Moore, "Introduction" to *Lawrence*, p. 10.
[5] "D. H. Lawrence," *New Yorker* (May 30, 1964), p. 136.

explains why she subtitled the work "An Unprofessional Study." Yet even the most cursory examination of the work yields an almost opposite impression. Not only does she undertake in less than one hundred pages to encompass the thought and art of an enormously productive and, at the time, critically scorned artist, but she does so with an obvious note of contempt and condescension toward the common critical principles: "One word about influences, since no study is supposed to be complete without it" (71); Lawrence's philosophy, she pointedly states at the outset, "was not a coolly constructed formula, an assemblage of theories fitting reasonably together" (13); repeatedly she emphasizes that one of Lawrence's characters does not fit into the "conventional world" of "normal people" (77-78).

In short, one comes to the conclusion that the assumption that *D. H. Lawrence: An Unprofessional Study* is a critical work, in the usual sense of the word, is based upon the *appearance* of the work and upon the premise that a *study* is by definition an objectively critical piece of work. Unfortunately, perhaps, one must describe this situation as extremely ironic. For central to Nin's "study" is first, the argument that there are two very different ideas as to what constitutes criticism and influence: just as there are two different ways to approach the world in which we live, so there are two ways to approach the world created by an artist; and just as there are two very different ways to measure the relationship between two people, so there are two ways to measure the relationships between one artist and another. And secondly, her "study" is concerned with demonstrating that the one way—the one upon which her work is structured—is infinitely better than the other—and this is the one upon which the present assumptions concerning her work are based.

> Scientists and philosophers who have gathered up all the observed facts about the life of man, and of the earth, stars and planets, and their laws, have told us that birth, life, disintegration, and renewal, is the cycle of the universe. But they were looking *out* from themselves; if they had looked *into* themselves, they would have observed the same cycles, as Lawrence did. Lawrence was not interested in the cosmos, and it is a mistake to read his books as great cosmic allegories. He was not interested in God in the abstract but in the gods that inhabited Somers' body (in *Kangaroo*) and that were his personal and individual possessions. Thus Lawrence reduced his universe strictly to what he felt and experienced in himself, but, precisely because he was so intensely personal, that reduced universe is as full and complete as any conceived by cosmic minds. Within the limits of this personal universe, then, by inward contemplation, he discovered the personally experienced cycle of birth, life, disintegration and renewal. (86)

That her interpretation of Lawrence's art and her terminology are critically inadequate, to say the least, is the first thing one should recognize, paradoxical as it may sound. For with the text before us, we now are in a position to raise the question of whether or not explication and exactitude are the purpose and method that govern the passage. More specifically one might ask, is it to explain Lawrence's practice that she sets up the contrast, is she literally referring to scientists, *or* are Lawrence and the scientist-philosopher being used as examples to explain the difference between two modes of perception, between "realism and reality"? Is she attempting to be critical and objective and failing, or is she deliberately operating according to poetic and subjective principles? Such questions, of course, cannot be answered except through extended analysis of the passage in question and the work in general; the reason for raising them at this point is to caution against "jumping to conclusions" and to explain the method adopted in the following pages. If one can demonstrate that the passage in question is an index to the concerns of the entire work, if one can show that the work is designed to express her specific theory rather than generally to explicate Lawrence's practice, then one must conclude that her book is not the usual type of "study." Technically, the method involves not stopping to identify the works of Lawrence from which she quotes but rather treating such passages as her use of his words to express her own ideas.

According to Nin, then, there is an outward and an inward way to perceive the fundamental patterns of life. Basically her argument relies upon the traditional concept of correspondence between the microcosm and macrocosm which psychoanalysis had updated and temporalized in the theory that ontogeny recapitulates phylogeny. But it is essentially as a justification of the inward mode that the theory engages her, as her dislike for "cosmic allegories" suggests, and the bulk of her "study" is concerned with demonstrating the inadequacy of the scientific method and the value of the poetic. Before we examine what she has to say in this respect, however, it is well to point out that her method is not that of the romantic subjectivist. She is not simply stating that rationalism is bad, but attempting to prove that a specific kind of personal response is better. Her subjectivity is not the kind that characterizes the critic who tries to be objective and fails but rather a method of "reasoning against reasoning" (88).

"Scientists and philosophers who have gathered up all the observed facts about the life of man" are faulted by Nin on three counts. "Observed facts" indicates the first area of inadequacy. A detached spectator, the scientist is concerned with the features of the visible world. Which would be fine, according to Nin, except that there is "an unknown world within the known" (22) and frequently the "truth [is] concealed under appearances" (34). Also, there are "other forgotten worlds buried in our memories" (101). Her argument, then, is not that objectivity is bad but that as employed by the scientists it is a limited mode of perception which can lead to faulty conclusions. The eye can focus only upon appearances, and appearances are frequently deceiving. For example, distinctions between modes of being are based not on the way things are but on the way they look.

What is " 'non-life' as compared particularly with our life of the mind and its activities" may be "life on another perhaps dimly remembered plane" (101). "The first analysis of an event or a person yields a certain aspect. If we look at it again, it has another face. *The further we progress in our reinterpretation, the more prismatic are the moods and the imaginings coordinating the facts differently each time.* People who want a sane, static, measurable world take the first aspect of an event or person and stick to it, with an almost self-protective obstinacy, or by a natural limitation of their imaginations" (32-33). The scientists of the literary world are the literalist reader and the realistic writer, neither of whom appreciates that "realism is thus merely a beginning, a basis" (108) and that the poetic artist "never means what is literally apparent" (27).

The statistical method is the second reason why the scientific mode is inadequate. Says the scientist, "A hundred cases have proved that the reason why you do this or that falls under such and such a category, and requires such a cure. It is in the catalogue" (88). But according to Nin this proves only that there are a hundred cases; "It makes one think of the whole class of authors who think that taking an inventory of the universe is really literature" (92). The catalogue is the book of the dead, the average, and therefore is applicable only to the unreal figure, the dead-to-life, the "monk": " *'Neither the blood nor the spirit spoke in them, only the law, the abstraction of the average. The infinite is positive and negative. But the average is only neutral. And the monks trod backwards and forwards down the line of neutrality'* " (75).

Only one philosopher and only one scientist escape Nin's general censure of the critical mentality, and when one discovers who they are one realizes that they are the exceptions that prove her rule. The first is Heraclitus, the Greek philosopher who first objected to the "scientific" approach and advocated "inward contemplation." In opposition to his contemporaries' passion for *historia,* for the collecting of quantities of facts, Heraclitus observed that "the learning of many things teacheth not understanding," and announced as his motto, "I sought for myself."[6] In similar fashion Nin argues for the "deepening or magnifying" imagination against the quantitative idea of experience: ". . . the imagination is a constant deformer. It needs to be, it must be, in order to be capable of extending from comparatively small happenings, in a comparatively short span of life. Otherwise to understand one thought, on [sic] feeling, we would have to go through a thousand experiences" (32). Better than multiple experiences is the multi-leveled experience, "And this is simply the *fundamental basis of poetic creation*": "The love and hate alternating in men and women, as in *Women*

---

[6] For a general discussion of Heraclitus' philosophy and his relation to his times see Werner Jaeger, *Paideia: The Ideals of Greek Culture,* translated from the Second German Edition by Gilbert Highet (New York, 1965), II, pp. 178–184.

in Love is due to the same profound sense of oscillation, of flux and reflux (Herakleitos), revulsions and convulsions, *mobility. The becoming always seething and fluctuating"* (32). In passing, one might notice the tripartite nature of the argument: the theory is Nin's, Heraclitus provides the authority and Lawrence the example.

The scientist who receives Nin's approbation is also one who had questioned the validity of the traditional attitude toward facts and formulae: "This seeming paradox, that in the final analysis positive meets negative, that eternal being and eternal non-being are the same, in the origin and in the issue, as well as in *time,* is one that has been the common property of all the great mystics, though sometimes less clearly expressed [.] The same paradox has been restated in terms of modern science in the conclusions of Einstein" (76). To Nin, the theory of relativity is the scientific expression of the differences between appearance and reality.

The passage does not end with the reference to Einstein, however, and in what follows we discover the last reason for her opposition to the scientific and her justification of the poetic: "It remained for Lawrence, however, to give mysticism a rebirth in terms which have the advantage both over the traditional mysticism and the abstractions of mathematics in that he made us feel the unity in this eternal paradox *through our senses"* (76). In short, even if one finds a formula or philosophy that "allows ample room for the unexpected, for 'the creative powers and impulses of men'" (87) it still is inadequate because it appeals only to the intellect and by definition cannot convey the felt quality of reality.

As was the case in her initial argument for correspondence between the inner and the outer, this reasoning against the value of abstract knowledge is not an essentially new idea; Sidney, to name but one champion of the poetic, had made a similar argument in his *Defense.* What is new is the character of the opposition—no longer the philosopher and the historian, but the psychologist and the novelist of ideas. "Lawrence's descriptions of the undercurrents of body and mind were but means of bringing to the surface many feelings that we do not sincerely acknowledge in ourselves. Freud and Jung have also done this, but they are essentially scientists and they are read with the detachment and objectivity of scientific research" (32-33). Lawrence, Freud, and Jung, then, are concerned with expressing the same idea; yet, according to Nin, whereas the theories of the psychoanalysts were accepted, "Lawrence was reviled for going so far" (33). Which leads her to conclude, "So it was not the truth, but the stirring, live quality of Lawrence's truth which upset people" (33). Through a similar negative approach she demonstrates the limitations of the abstract and the power of the sensuous in fiction: "Besides the scientists there were novelists like André Gide and Aldous Huxley who had left nothing unexplored. But Huxley and Gide traveled with the intellect and with that upper strata [sic] in the head, and therefore as they went along we were *hit in our heads,* and the experience took on a scientific aspect, became pure abstract knowledge" (33). And again, according to Nin, although "there is nothing more devastating to ordinary standards of value than pages of *L'Immoraliste* and pages of Huxley's *Point Counterpoint* [sic], it was not against them but against Lawrence that "society rose bitterly." And again the reason lies in the difference between scientific and poetic language: *"Lawrence had been unforgivably persuasive.* He had not only thought about everything but he had felt everything . . ." (33-34). Because of its mode of expression, then, the scientific method is limited: " 'Real knowledge comes out of the whole corpus . . .' " (20).

Because appearances are deceiving, because the average is an unreal figure, and because formulae appeal only to the intellect, Nin finds the scientific method an unsatisfactory mode of operation. Her point of departure, of course, is a humanistic concept of what is valuable, and her presentation is that of the poet rather than of the logician; but within this framework it must be admitted that her arguments are self-supporting, anti-rational but not irrational.

Similarly, in championing the personal perspective she does not romantically plead for mindless response but reasonably argues for the validity of a specific kind of subjectivity. The personal mode is not an unconsciously "closed mind" but a deliberately restricted perspective; it is not simply feeling but the objective evaluation of emotion that is involved; and it is not the satisfaction of the ego but the "personally experienced cycle" that is the goal. And again, the rationale for such an inward turning is not radical, at least not to us in the twentieth century.

Her initial justification of the personal, we have repeated, is the old idea of correspondence; her specific argument for the validity of the subjective is related to the modernization of this theory, that is the reversal of the old idea of the relationship between the mind and object. The reason why the macrocosm corresponds to the microcosm is that man is the creator of the universe, or conversely, that the universe as we know it is a projection of our own minds. For example, using Lawrence's *Twilight in Italy,* she notices that "Christ on the Cross is altered each time by the vision of the carver": "One Christ is elegant, brave, keen. Death is important but it must be elegant. Another Christ is weak and sentimental. Self-pity has been expressed by the carver. Other people must have His death pictured with sensationalism, and much blood. Death for them is approached with violence" (73). Similarly, the Madonna and Child is essentially a reflection of man's "vision of himself" (40): "So man's experience was: 'himself as Christ-child, standing on the lap of a Virgin Mother'" (39). And the proof that the "'great religious images are only images of our own experience'" (39) is that when man's experiences change so does his image of reality, as the difference between the pre- and post-war ideals indicate (39). Which is, specifically and generally, why a new idea of reality is in order: " 'Now man cannot live without some vision of himself. But still less can he live with a vision that is not true to his own inner experience and inner feeling' " (40).

And what is true of religion is true of all our images of the external world, as Nin makes doubly clear in her discussion of Lawrence's "political" novel, *Kangaroo*. " 'Poor Richard Lovat'," Nin quotes from the work, " 'wearied himself to death struggling with the problem of himself and calling it Australia' " (92); but then she goes one step further, " ' The absence of inner meaning,' which is in Australia, is for the moment in a pessimistic Lawrence" (92). Out of context this sounds like the all too frequent biographical interpretation of Lawrence's fiction; taken in context it suggests her uncritical use of Lawrence as a practical example of her own thesis: "Kangaroo is given to a kind of cosmic love somewhat like Whitman's. Somers is suspicious of cosmic love. For creation begins and ends at the core of individuality . . ." (97).

While admittedly a more poetic version, Nin's argument for the validity of subjectivity, then, belongs to the tradition initiated by Kant, developed by Emerson and other philosophical romantics, and given definite expression by Cassirer in the twentieth century. "Irresponsible" as she may seem to the reader who is "hot for certainties," in short, she is not without support; her emphasis upon the "conception of the multiplicity of God, that is, many gods in every man, and the conception of individual gods as individual possessions" (43) is basically a poeticization of the theory that the only knowable reality is in the perceiver and the perception rather than in any external *ding an sich*. In the literary world, this "Copernican revolution" was wrought essentially by Henry James—which may best explain the epigraph Nin selected for her "study": " '. . . The critic's task is to compare a work with its own concrete standard of truth . . .'."

An extension of this revaluation of reality is Nin's argument for the inclusion of two modes of understanding excluded by the scientists. "The heart has reasons which the reason cannot understand," wrote Pascal. "Why should not an impulse be wise, or wisdom be impulsive," she asks at the beginning of her "study" (20). By impulse she means significantly both instinct—biological response—and intuition—psychic comprehension. And when later in the work she answers her own question she uses the terms interchangeably. "An intuition cannot be explained rationally either to others or even to one's self. . . . The instinct is there: sometimes even to justify it, in a frantic effort to give a rational explanation, one is invented, which adds to the confusion" (94). The reason science rules out impulse, thus, is that its mode of expression is definitively rational, and—making a virtue of this limitation—that it has defined wisdom as intellection. But, argues Nin, precisely because instinct and intuition are non-rational and non-intellectual they are more to be trusted than the intelligence, which is "a juggler, an adroit juggler who can make everything balance and fall right" (18); simply because impulse is beyond mental control it is "undeceived, undeceivable" (18); exactly because it operates with a "pure, profound disregard of appearances" (17) it is more in tune with reality than cognition which operates through the eye. In similar fashion, one recalls, Wagner had argued for the supremacy of music because as a non-cognitive art-form it put the listener in direct contact with the world beyond. And finally, as Cassirer had argued for the mythic modality,[7] if reality is located in the subject and mode of perception, then the universe perceived through intuition must be granted as much validity as that "*conceived* by cosmic minds" (86, italics mine).

But, it must be emphasized, to Nin intuition is not an end in itself. "There is nothing more discouraging than a truth perceived by intuition" (95) because of the difficulty in formulating it; "What a task—to make instinct clear to the mind!" (94). Nevertheless, it must be done. Plato's caveman must return and tell; it is Schopenhauer's artist, not his saint, who resembles Nin's "poet." *Kangaroo,* according to Nin, is a "tortured" work because Lawrence "stuck to the inarticulate instinct" and struggled for expression. Why, she asks, does he do this, why does he persist: "And all the while, what is the reason for Lawrence's complication-producing mechanism? It is the business of the creator. He was to write precisely this book *Kangaroo, a reflection of all such complications.* Other men overtaken by the same spirit of intuition could then clarify this intuition and be spared much of the revolution. The madness of Lawrence was to set a precedent, so that other people might realized [sic] the sanity of their own feelings, proved by the conclusions of *Kangaroo*" (94). Intuition, then, is a personal means to a universal end: "Work or creation of any intensity has always produced a state of excessive sensibility. The trances of the Hindus, the exaltations of the Christian martyrs, the fever of creation and thought have all been equally abnormal." But, "It was during such abnormal states that there appeared visions which were afterwards used by normal men in normal living" (70). In short, it is not transcendence, but "transcendental definitions" (17) that justify the intuitive approach; subjectivity of this kind is paradoxically the means to the highest kind of objectivity. To apprehend the primitive mentality it is necessary to think like one, but to appreciate this condition, ironically, one must be extremely sophisticated: in *Twilight*

---

[7] See especially Ernst Cassirer, "Introduction: The Problem of a Philosophy of Mythology," in *The Philosophy of Symbolic Forms,* II, translated by Ralph Manheim (New Haven and London, 1968), pp. 1-26. One might also note at this point that in 1921 Cassirer had published *Zur Einsteinchen Relativatstheorie,* one of the first applications of Einstein's theories to literature and culture, and a more likely "source" of Nin's knowledge of the theory of relativity than the writings of the scientist.

in Italy, Lawrence "stops in admiration of an old woman who is spinning, and closes his brain, silences the upper strata, and watches he [sic] with 'the open eyes of the breast,' seeing her with the vision of the body; and so he understands her. He broods then on the fact that though she does not *realize herself* she *possesses herself,* and wonders then if we cannot possess ourselves without consciousness. But it is precisely Lawrence's consciousness which makes him create the old woman for us" (74). Or again, in Lawrence's poem *Fish* she explains the process in the following brief manner: "Here it is almost as if he were in a trance in which he communicates with another plane of existence. Approaching with wary sensitivity he leaves us with a completely objective image" (100). But it is Lawrence's *New Heaven and Earth* that is for her the best example and consequently the best example we can use to summarize this aspect of her theory.

According to her interpretation, the work opens with the speaker in the posture of the scientist, looking outward at the world only to discover that it is not an objective reality but the projection of himself that he is observing:

> The poem begins with a simple description of his "old world," the everyday world of which he had been too much a part:
>
> > "I was so weary of the world,
> > I was so sick of it,
> > Everything was tainted with myself,
> >
> > . . . .
> >
> > . . . it was all tainted with myself,
> > I knew it all to start with
> > Because it was all myself."
>
> He had reached the extreme of self-consciousness: (102)

But instead of the romantic *cul de sac* this subjectivity is simply the first stage in a new awareness:

> Living that everyday life, letting his mind associate and merge with the world's mind and its activities, he realizes that he had become an inseparable fragment of that world. So long as he should identify himself with that world he was responsible of [sic] it; all was in him, and he in all. He was its creator until he should create something new. This is a recurrence of Lawrence's idea, with which we are already familiar, of the evolution of the universe reduced to terms of our individual souls:
>
> > "When I saw the torn dead I knew it was my own torn dead body
> > It was all me, I had done it all in my own flesh.
> >
> > . . . .
> >
> > I was the God and the creation at once;
> > Creator, I looked at my creation;
> > Created, I looked at myself, the creator." (102-103)

Subjectivity here is at once the problem and the solution; if the world as man knows it is his own creation, by surrendering his personality man can

24

destroy it: "So the creator must die, he must bury himself, which was his world, his creation" (103). And in doing so, he achieves ultimate objectivity, "he discovers a new world":

> ". . . that which was verily not me . . .
>
> . . . .
>
> It was the unknown."

New Heaven and Earth is an allegory of Lawrence's wide cycle of experience. Widening and widening the boundaries of experience and understanding he inevitably reached the breaking point in his own disintegration through which in turn he touched the secret mysteries of the earth and so found new sources of strength and deeper life: (104)

According to Nin, then, "inward contemplation" is justified because—and when—it leads from the personal beyond to the universal and then back to the concrete (or personal) universal, the work of art: "For creation begins and ends at the core of individuality and it is only by merging into art (like the sum total of Lawrence's work) that it goes to serve the universe" (97). Thus instead of simple subjectivity the method involves a double objectivity, which explains her criticism of two seemingly opposite types of writer, on the one hand, and the way she handles Lawrence's work, on the other. The social critic like the romantic is too subjective, too personally involved to see things in their proper—their atemporal and impersonal—perspective: "A great deal of rebellious, combative thought misses ultimate truth. Great writers have generally found themselves only when they have freed themselves of their antagonisms" (70); the "sentimental poets" are prone to use "animal life or nature to illustrate some human principle or emotion. And then worlds and metaphors are mixed" and "abstractions are made no clearer" (102). In contrast, the true artist is the man who both looks at himself and at his times objectively and who projects himself, not impulsively onto nature, but deliberately into his art: "However much he puts himself into his books, he is above all an artist since he can stand off from and observe critically even his most passionate feelings and convictions" (80). Since Lawrence is her example of such a self-expressive artist, she frequently interchanges his name with those of his characters, but she never reduces his art to autobiography and repeatedly castigates those who entertain such a literalist and subjective idea of the artistic process: "Since his world is the enlargement of his own gigantic imagination, out to see and to experience all, the characters have their roots in reality, but they are soon disassociated from familiar moulds and absorbed by Lawrence. He is at work on such a vast, almost impersonal comprehension, that realities are not sufficient: he must use symbols" (16). All varieties of personal experience, in short, are means to an end rather than goals in themselves; art is a mode of self-expression, but a deliberate rather than an unconscious projection; organic form does not demonstrate that the artist has lost control but rather that he has finally succeeded in objectifying his intuitions to the extent that he is able to wander as a creator through his own creation: "He does not spare us . . . the long moments of his watchfulness, which often yield nothing. He is not chiselling to give us a work of formal art. He is living and progressing within his own book" (68).

At the centre of Nin's "study" of D. H. Lawrence, to summarize quickly, there is an argument of "a new way of knowing" (44) which is presented in terms of a demonstration of the limitations of the "old"—the realistic and rationalistic—way and through an explanation of the ultimate objectivity of the intuitive and poetic method. Our concern now must be with the implications of such a theory, and it is here that a crucial decision with respect to the nature of the work must be made. To explain: the critic who uses an artist to expound a personal thesis is by academic standards a "bad" critic; if Anais Nin was attempting to write a traditional "study" of Lawrence then she has failed, and no amount of special pleading for isolated insights can stay the judgment. If she is operating upon a different concept of criticism, however, then to fault her—or to praise her—in conventional terms is as absurd as to charge a poet with not writing novels. Supporting the first supposition is the generic word of the title, "study"; destroying it is the qualifying adjective, "unprofessional," and the repeated allusion in the work to what might be called the modern prototype of subjective criticism, D. H. Lawrence's own *Studies in Classic American Literature*.

According to Nin, Lawrence is not attempting objectively to analyze American writers but rather he is concerned with the material this literature affords for expression of his own theories: "Just as in *Studies in Classical American Literature* Lawrence brought his entire individual philosophy to bear upon criticism, so in considering psychology he had to give us a personal interpretation" (87). In his essay on Edgar Allan Poe, it is not Poe's but "Lawrence's experience of disintegration of the soul" that is being described; it is not its meaning for Poe but "its meaning for him" that is the subject of the essay (86). To quote from Lawrence's essay on Whitman is to present in a double sense "his essential message" (71). In short, instead of a critical survey of American literature, "In *Classical Studies in American Literature* [Lawrence] gives a summary of his own conclusions" (47). To Nin, then, American literature is like any other "experience" to Lawrence; it is the material toward which he directs his intuition, and his study thus becomes, like his art, a projection of his personal response. Instead of objective and analytic, criticism thus becomes subjective and creative.

That this concept of criticism accords perfectly with her theoretical defense of the "inward" mode is obvious; however, before demonstrating that her "study" is a similar type of criticism, that like Lawrence's it is a deliberately creative and subjective one, that Lawrence's art is to her what

American literature was to Lawrence, it will be well to consider what a professional critic has to say concerning Lawrence's criticism.

In an article entitled "Criticism as Rage," Richard Foster observes that Lawrence "is virtually unheard as a critic," mainly because "he participates in an odd kind of subtradition of his own made up of intellectual renegades, of violently creative minds, of brilliant and angry men whom the ordering techniques of the historian never quite succeed in assimilating into the homogeneous textures of their 'periods'." Such men he continues, are not simply iconoclasts, because "they are makers as well as breakers. . . . *They are never specialists, always instinctively amateurs.*" Then turning to Lawrence specifically, he surveys some characteristic statements, and goes on to observe, "This partial and hasty catalogue of his literary opinions illustrates no more, of course, than that Lawrence as a critic was subjective, capricious, dogmatic. It fails to show two important things. One is that, as I have said, his criticism is also art," and second, "that, spontaneous and subjective as his critical performance may seem, Lawrence knew quite consciously—that is to say, theoretically and philosophically—what he expected of art, and he knew how to use these expectations as principles, even as the basis and threshold for a general *method* of criticism peculiarly his own."[8] The reason for introducing these comments is not to demonstrate that Nin was accurate in her interpretation of Lawrence, but rather to suggest that radical as it may appear her "study" does belong to a tradition; that is, everything that Foster says about Lawrence's criticism of American literature applies equally well to Nin's "study" of Lawrence. It is "instinctively amateur," deliberately subjective, and organized according to a personal theory. Above all, her "criticism is also art."

To begin, one might notice the variant repetitions of the phrase "Lawrence's world" and the concrete manner in which she describes her "approach": "The world D. H. Lawrence created cannot be entered through the exercise of one faculty alone" (13); "Reading Lawrence should be a pursuit of his intuitions to the limit of their possibilities, a penetration of his world . . ." (14). To Nin, in short, the fictional world is as real as the phenomenal; reading is as much an experience as any physical action; criticism consequently involves the same modes that one uses to perceive the world in which one lives. Like the phenomenal world, the fictional one also has its realisms and its realities: "The most characteristic attitude of the true Lawrence is a state of high seriousness and lyrical intensity" (13); "In considering Lawrence's poetry it is necessary to set to one side that part which is merely expository and didactic, where he was repeating ideas better expressed in his prose and belonging more properly to prose, as distinct from the relatively few poems in which the true poet in him spoke

---

[8] Richard Foster, "Criticism as Rage: D. H. Lawrence," in *A D. H. Lawrence Miscellany*, ed. Harry T. Moore (Carbondale, 1959), pp. 312–325 (emphases mine).

naturally and spontaneously" (98); *Twilight in Italy* is a "book to be considered by itself because it contains a Lawrence particularly true to himself" (73). And just as the critic of the phenomenal world should be concerned with ultimate realities, according to Nin, so the literary critic should not waste time on non-essentials: "It is unnecessary to dwell on the occasional retrogression—the imperfections and technical weaknesses, since they are quite unimportant in an ultimate valuation of his work" (37). To the critic, it is hardly necessary to add, the imperfections of an artist demand almost as much consideration as his perfections, at least in any objective analysis.

The structure of Nin's "study" similarly indicates the creative nature of the work. We have seen that the problem of perception is literally and figuratively at the centre of her work. The first and last sentences of the work provide the perfect frame for such a focus: " 'The business of the mind is first and foremost the pure joy of knowing and comprehending, the pure joy of consciousness' " (13) is the way her "study" begins; " 'For me it's the only thing in the world . . .' " (110) is the way it ends. Both sentences are Lawrence's, but the eclecticism is Nin's.

Supporting this thematic structure, furthermore, are both an imagistic and a narrative pattern. In "The Approach to D. H. Lawrence's World," Nin announces that we are about "to make a prodigious voyage. It is going to be a prodigious voyage because he surrenders fully to experience, lets it flow through him . . ." (14). Later she reminds the reader, "If we want to make the labyrinthian voyage . . . if we want to go along with him, very well. He is too busy, too intent, just now, to entertain us" (68). Thus the anonymous reviewer who condemned the work as a "long breathy gush" was insensitively correct;[9] the work does create the impression of a *"fleuve,"* to use the word Nin later selects to describe the structure of her fiction, but it is deliberately so designed; her goal is to create the impression of a mind wandering through a fictional world, of a sensitive reader attempting to chart his way through his responses. ". . . did we not make the labyrinthian voyage with Proust?" she asks; the reference perhaps provides a clue to the genre in which one should place her work—the stream-of-consciousness fiction. "Layers of obscure memories were roused unexpectedly by the smell of a bun, or the lacing of a shoe. No one knew by what coordination a memory would rise out of oblivion and illumine the darkness of our world" (67); in similar fashion a line, a word from Lawrence's fiction impels a train of thought on the part of Nin. For example, one section begins, *"Hierarchy.* A hierarchy is a form, a formality. For the first time Lawrence insists on a form: there must be a hierarchy" (55). At other times a quotation is introduced like a thought out of the clear blue sky: " '. . . Man

---

[9] "D. H. Lawrence," *New Yorker* (May 30, 1964), p. 136.

is lop-sided on the side of the angels . . .' " (66). As this example also suggests, the use of ellipses creates a simultaneous impression of spontaneity and continuous flow, of a journey through a labyrinth.

Like Lawrence's *Fantasia of the Unconscious,* which has also been misunderstood because approached with rationalistic rather than poetic criteria,[10] Nin's work also evidences a narrative pattern; indeed, and again like Lawrence's work, one of the oldest:

> In the beginning, the idyllic beginning, when difficulties are felt only through a half-dim consciousness, Lawrence has ample freedom to observe the background, and we have the classical, almost naive surface landscape painting of the [sic] *White Peacock.*
>
> As Lawrence the poet evolves, the background becomes ominous, as in *Sons and Lovers.* Further on it becomes symbolical, as in *Twilight in Italy.* There, while descriptions of nature are richer than ever, it is their reflection in the mind and feelings which becomes more essential. As he discovers the universe and pierces the crust of the earth with his personal vision, the background becomes more and more symbolical. (15)

Nin's Lawrence, it will be obvious, is an Adamic figure, born into a world of appearances, who redeems himself and it by becoming a poet. "First of all he asks us to begin at the beginning of the world with him. By his own questions, put as seriously as a child's, and with a child's obstinacy, he will take each man back to the beginning of the world, as if each had to settle it all for himself, begin his own world, find his god" (16). Keeping this Edenic motif in focus throughout the work are a pair of contrasting images: the cold, superficial eye and the warm vision rooted in the body: "Lawrence approaches his characters not in a state of intellectual lucidity but in one of *intuitional reasoning.* His observation is not *through the eye but through the central physical vision*—or instinct" (18). "Lawrence believed that the feelings of the body, from its most extreme impulses to its smallest gesture, are the warm root for true vision, and from that warm root can we truly grow" (19); "Whatever way he turns he must make sex mystical, part of his religion, a fundamental part of it. His religion is to have roots, marvelous, *warm roots*" (42). Nin's "study," in short, is a "literary" *Paradise Lost* and *Regained.* It begins in the fashion of Genesis; in the middle is a chapter entitled "The Return to the Primitive" (47-48); and it ends with her example of the perfect literary reunion of realism and reality: "In *Lady Chatterley's Lover* Lawrence's work reaches its climax. Paradoxically it is at once his fleshiest and his most mystical work" (107); "If, to some, his work is nothing but crude realism, to others who know poetry it is more than that: the prose is lyrical as well as sensual, the descriptions full of sensitiveness as well as crudeness, of beauty as well as

---

[10] See my "The Beginning and the End: D. H. Lawrence's *Psychoanalysis* and *Fantasia*," *Dalhousie Review,* LII (Summer, 1972), pp. 251–265.

obscenity. A vigorous and impetuous style carries the weight of intense physical and imaginative emotions and in the end unites them in a brilliant fusion of physical-mysticism" (108).

A final way of suggesting that Nin is deliberately using rather than attempting to explicate Lawrence is to draw attention to the nature of her eclecticism. *The Plumed Serpent,* one of Lawrence's longest and certainly a major work, is never mentioned; *The Princess,* a story, is given a separate chapter. Her "analysis" and the fact that this "title" was the one which her friends bestowed upon her may explain why: *"The Princess* is the fairytale of mysterious individuality. When her father says to her: 'People and the things they say and do . . . it is all nothing. Inside everybody there is another creature, a demon which doesn't care at all. You peel away the things they say and do and feel. . . . And in the middle of everybody there is a green demon which you can't peel away. And this green demon never changes, and it doesn't care at all about the things that happen to the outside leaves of the person . . .' "(105). Similarly, she devotes a chapter to the subject of "Women," and introduces Lawrence's *Autobiographical Sketch* essentially in order to make the following comment about the artistic personality: "He puts it all down to class divisions, himself, but it is not so. He is deluded by the inordinate class distinctions existing in England, which do form a real blind barrier between men. But it is easy to see that he is isolated simply because he is an individualist and a creator. . . . He did not know it, but *he was making a class for himself,* for others somewhat like him" (91).

In 1930 Stephen Potter published a work entitled *D. H. Lawrence: A First Study;* in 1932 Nin published a work which she entitled *D. H. Lawrence: An Unprofessional Study.* In view of the preceding discussion of her work, one begins to suspect that it was not to apologize but to *distinguish* her "study" from the professional variety that she appended the subtitle; hers is an "unprofessional study" by design and not by default. Like Lawrence in *Fantasia,* she is deliberately announcing her uncritical bias: " 'I am not a proper archeologist, [sic] nor an anthropologist, nor an ethnologist. I am no scholar of any sort. . . . I proceed by intuition' " (71).

But that her work is essentially creative rather than critical does not mean that it has no critical value. And again, it is her own theory that best explains the seeming paradox. "It is an old philosophic truth," she observes, that "an experience, provided it is lived with intensity and sincerity, often leads out of itself into its opposite" (107). Just as, we have seen, the subjective and intuitive can lead back to objectivity, so her impressions of Lawrence frequently do coincide with objective criticism of his work. But the point that needs emphasis is that her work should not be evaluated upon these grounds, just as any work of art should not be evaluated in terms of its historical or autobiographical accuracy. *D. H. Lawrence: An*

Unprofessional Study should be approached in the same manner that one approaches Lawrence's *Studies in Classic American Literature*—as the deliberate use of fiction to express a personal theory. Whatever insights result from the procedure should be considered as secondary and incidental.

In having explored the nature of Nin's criticism of Lawrence, we have also generally confronted the subject of her indebtedness; for if her "study" is essentially self-expressive, then the question of influence becomes more a question of development. However, since the subject is central to most discussions of her work and since she herself specifically touches upon the problem, some further words are in order.

That the critic who omitted her "study" from his discussion of her creative work should repeatedly attempt to demonstrate how "profoundly influenced" she was by Lawrence does not come as a surprise when one examines his idea of influence.[11] "Stella," we are told, "is probably the most Lawrentian of all Miss Nin's narratives, not merely in its subject, but also in the rendering of particular scenes. Take the following, for instance, which might easily have been written by Lawrence." After quoting a passage he continues, "There is the same emotional exaggeration, the same tendency toward melodrama, which we find in Lawrence. Or take this, which might almost have come from *Lady Chatterley's Lover*." After quoting again, he goes on, "Not the best of Miss Nin, certainly, any more than similar passages are the best of Lawrence, but even here it is interesting to note that she has not been content with making a merely realistic observation but has, through the use of the metaphor 'calendar of their love,' lifted it out of the category of the purely physical—something that Lawrence does not always do. Nevertheless, the affinity is unmistakable."[12] Undoubtedly, the motive for such a procedure is laudable, but the effect is extremely negative. Not only does it create the impression that Nin is a derivative writer but also that she is second-rate and unable to stand without buttressing. But more to the specific point, the comparisons are so general that any number of writers could be substituted for Lawrence, and this leads one to conclude that the reason for using Lawrence is based, on the one hand, upon the knowledge that Nin's first work was a "study" of his work, and on the other, upon the idea that contact between two writers constitutes grounds for influence. In short, we are faced with a mechanical idea of the relationship between one writer and another, just as earlier we were faced with the objective concept of criticism. And aside from this general orientation, in the specific case of Nin, the error arises from considering her first work as critical rather than as creative and impressionistic. If Nin's Lawrence is not the objective Lawrence that scholarship has discovered, then to talk about his influence upon her writing may be as un-

---

[11] Evans, *Anaïs Nin*, p. 28.
[12] *Ibid.*, pp. 97-98.

profitable as to talk about her indebtedness to an artist she never knew; but to talk about the way her later work develops from this early "study" is quite another matter.

A few examples will bring the issue into clearer focus. "Lawrence does not create what we generally understand by a 'character'," observes Nin. "He does not give such a clear outline because the personages in his books are symbolical; he is more preoccupied with the states of consciousness and with subconscious acts, moods, and reactions" (26). "The key to his characters," she concludes, "or the simplest way of understanding them, is to think of them as artists" (26). Whether or not this is an accurate assessment of Lawrence's practice is at best debatable, since while most Lawrence scholars would agree that his characters are different from those found in the well-made novel, many would not agree that his characters are so allegorically fashioned, or that they do not bear "a resemblance to those we know" (26). On the other hand, the characters in Nin's later fiction not only have the sensitivity of artists and demonstrate "the laws of subconscious actions" (26) but, as we shall see, they literally are artists and act out roles in a psychic drama. In short, Nin's statement more accurately describes what she will do than what Lawrence has done. And this is not to commit the fallacy of anticipation, but rather to suggest the subjectivity and creativity of her criticism and the advisability of treating her later fiction as a development from this early work rather than as a consequence of Lawrence's influence.

"Modern psychology," she herself emphasizes, has "told us that no feeling can be awakened in us unless we have the roots of it in ourselves; no ideas can be put into our heads, they can only be developed when the seed of them is already growing in us" (109). The statement is an excellent modernization of Melville's "shock of recognition," which is the poetic, in contrast to the mechanical concept of influence. What one artist discovers in another is not something new but a confirmation of his own ideas. It is Cassirer's creative perception, not Locke's *tabula rasa* that is involved. "Whatever Lawrence owed to Hardy and Dostoevsky he transformed and recreated. Whatever influenced him served merely to illumine a part of his own self-contained world" (72). Whatever Nin owed to Lawrence she also transformed and re-created.

"'Commandments should fade as flowers do'," Nin quotes at the end of her introductory chapter. "'The secret of all life is obedience: obedience to the urge that arises in the soul, the urge that is life itself, urging us to new gestures, new embraces, new emotions, new combinations, new creations'" (14). Her "study" of Lawrence, I have tried to demonstrate, is such a "new creation," and consequently needs to be approached as such rather than according to the old commandments of criticism.

III

☆ ☆ ☆ ☆ ☆

Karma, Tropism, and Fixation

In the September, 1937, issue of *The Booster*, a magazine with which Anaïs Nin was associated in an editorial capacity, the following "manifesto" appears: "In the main *The Booster* will be a contraceptive against the self-destructive spirit of the age. We are not interested in political line-ups, nor social panaceas, nor economic nostrums. We believe the world will always be a trying place to live in, but a good place just the same. We are *for* rather than *against*."[1] This statement is enlightening in two ways: first, it implies, through the nature of the protest, the type of novel that was popular at the time when she began writing, the proletarian novel; second, it indicates that Anaïs Nin was not alone in her objections to the themes and attitudes of "the lost generation." In turn, these observations help to explain why rightly and wrongly her fiction has been described as "narrow."[2]

One aspect of her early affinity to Lawrence is that—according to her—he recognized the limited value of social criticism and consequently pursued more profound themes: "Had Lawrence detached himself so much from current human problems that he could not be understood by the intelligent men of his time?" she asks with a hint of irony after quoting Middleton Murry's admission that he could not understand what Lawrence was about; and then she goes on to answer, "Precisely that. He detached himself from the current human problems which current writers could fathom" (*Lawrence*, 22). And later, in her discussion of *Kangaroo*—one begins to understand why this most political of Lawrence's works is given so much negative attention—she considers the difference between two kinds of fictional material: *"What is going through an experience?* Sometimes it is living it out in action, but *sometimes it is denying it.* That is one kind of experience. Lawrence does not take part in the revolution, but he takes part in a terrific struggle with himself. . . . To withhold, and to let the experience die, and lie there is one thing. But to withhold because of a profounder inner revolution is to deny one experience for another of greater importance, that is all" (*Lawrence*, 93). For "revolutions," she concludes, "are better in-

---

[1] "Editorial," in *The Booster* (September, 1937), p. 5.

[2] According to Evans, "Though her sincerity is unquestionable, her scope is narrow—dangerously narrow, perhaps. . . . There are whole areas of human experience—and important areas—about which she has not written, and perhaps could not have. These are severe limitations." See *Anaïs Nin*, p. 198.

wardly fought in ourselves than *en masse*. The masses can throw bombs, but they cannot create a soul" (*Lawrence,* 94).

An aristocratic concept of the artist because of a moral concept of the function of art is then the general reason why Anaïs Nin turns from the immediate and mundane scene. And it is this rationale that Elizabeth Hardwick, in a comment typical of those who find Nin "narrow," fails to take into consideration: "Anaïs Nin," she writes, "shuns the real world as if it had a bad reputation. This elegant snobbishness seems not designed to get her on in good society, but to allow her to sneak away to the psychological underworld. . . ."[3] But Nin's inwardness is not a matter of escaping from responsibility but of focusing upon the spiritual causes rather than upon the social consequences. It is a question of values and perspective.

"While we refuse to organize the confusions within us we will never have an objective understanding of what is happening outside."[4] According to Nin, the individual himself must be put in order before any mass reorganization is possible, or as William Burford writes in support of her focus on personal rather than political, social, or ideological themes, "We can only begin to understand our culture by understanding the individuals who both made and are made by that culture."[5] This does not mean that Anaïs Nin removes her characters from the social scene and studies them *in vacuo,* but that she takes the individual's view of society rather than society's view of the individual as her point of reference. And since she views the individual as "man" rather than as an economic integer or the smallest unit in a social structure, the order that she is primarily interested in is the natural order, man's relationship to nature in the larger context, his inner or psychological organization in the smaller.

But by turning inward to get at the origin of social problems Nin is not attempting to provide a psychoanalytic reading of history, although the cursory reader of her criticism may come away with such an impression, and not without justification. All too frequently she uses a psychoanalytic term loosely and gratuitously. Not to excuse her, it is important to point out, however, that her motive is not to turn literature into psychoanalysis but to technically modernize the critical vocabulary of psychological literature. To explain, in *On Writing* she outspokenly observes that "we are suffering from a collective neurosis."[6] The reader, possibly with annoyance, is reminded of the early N. O. Brown's psycho-literary study, *Life Against Death,* and remembers that Nin herself was a student of Otto Rank, who began his career as a disciple of Freud. But while Nin's diagnosis sounds

---

[3] Elizabeth Hardwick, "Fiction Chronicle," *Partisan Review,* XV (June, 1948), p. 706. The tone of this review is best indicated by Hardwick's gratuitous observation that Nin was "the sickly child of distinguished parents" (p. 705).

[4] *On Writing,* p. 18.

[5] Burford, p. 9.

[6] *On Writing,* p. 17.

Freudian, its implications are essentially poetic rather than clinical, and it is in the company of the later N. O. Brown and the recanted Rank that she belongs.[7]

"Neurosis," as she very broadly defines the term, is "simply a form of protest against an unnatural life."[8] It is the ironically natural consequence of civilization and consequently is discoverable in the histories of all ages and peoples. Psychoanalysis did not invent the situation; it only attached a label and described the problem more precisely and scientifically. As a conscientious modern, Nin uses the new term in her critical writing but retains the old and more comprehensive meaning in her fiction. The symptom of the neurotic condition in the modern world is "the absence, or failure of relationships between men and women"; the cause, a severance of the relationship between man and nature, both physically—through mechanization—and psychologically—through intellectualization. But the situation is not hopeless, even "though there is no going back."[9]

As Nin sees it, woman, because she is more elemental than man, has still retained her relationship with nature. Relying on the traditional and poetic division between man and woman as head *versus* heart, she sees the relationship between woman and nature as a complement to the world of man and the mind. Paralleling the role of God, the spiritual Father, is Nature, the archetypal Mother; corresponding to Man, the intellectual saviour, is Woman, the instinctual redeemer. Ideally, the feminine balances the masculine trinity: "The core of woman is her relationship to man" on the one side and to nature on the other; the core of man is his relationship to woman on the one side and to the spirit on the other.

However, as she begins to examine this role of woman as link between man and nature she finds that the modern woman is no longer capable of performing her essential function "because of her tendency to imitate man and adopt his goals."[10] Before she can focus her concern on what might be, then, Anaïs Nin feels she must first diagnose what is: "It is necessary to return to the origin of the confusion." For this reason she limits her theme not only to the problem of woman, but to the problem of the neurotic woman. "Man appears only partially," she explains, "because for the woman at war with herself he can only appear thus, not as an entity."[11]

But because the focus is on woman does not mean that the Nin novels have nothing to say to the male reader. Man is as much to blame for woman's neurosis as she herself is "because of [his] fear of complete contact with nature." Thus, although she does not discuss the problem of man

[7] Both Brown and Rank began as Freudians, but as *Love's Body* and *Art and Artist* demonstrate, both recognized and consequently departed from the reductive direction of psychoanalysis.

[8] *On Writing*, p. 18.

[9] *Ibid.*, p. 18.

[10] *Ibid.*, p. 17.

[11] "Prologue" to *Ladders*, p. [ii].

directly, she does so implicitly. As one of her more perceptive male critics observes: "Here if you like is the commentary of a sensitive and percipient Eve on the inadequacies of the eternal Adam."[12]

In its broadest aspects the theme of Anaïs Nin's creative writing is "woman at war with herself." The garden and the mirror as thematic symbols refer to the two directions in which this struggle can lead, the positive one of creativity and the negative one of destruction. But subordinate and central to each of these patterns is the third controlling idea, the theme of karma. An analysis of it must precede other considerations.

"Can't one throw anything away forever?" asks the narrator in one of Nin's short stories, "Ragtime." In reply a group of ragpickers chant the following jingle:

> Nothing is lost but it changes
> into the new string old string
> in the new bag old bag
> in the new pan old tin
> in the new shoe old leather
> in the new silk old hair
> in the new hat old straw
> in the new man the child
> and the new not new
> the new not new
> the new not new. (*Bell,* 58)

The "new not new" is the basic idea of karma. The word and theory, of course, are not original with Anaïs Nin. Nor does she accept the doctrine without adapting it to her purposes. But as the jingle itself explains, she realizes that an old theory provides the best basis for a new expression.

Karma, an extension of the Buddhist doctrine of Reincarnation, is the Oriental version of the Christian admonition: "Whatsoever a man soweth that shall he reap." But there is one essential difference between the two explanations of spiritual cause and effect, a difference that makes the Oriental doctrine a much better vehicle for Nin's purposes. To the traditional Christian, life on earth terminates in an essentially static heaven or hell, and since the latter is usually regarded as an analogue to our penological practices and the former as an abstract state of beatitude, the punishment of hell is usually described as physical discomfort and psychic isolation regardless of the specific nature of the crime; and reward is usually pictured as amorphous heavenly joy regardless of the specific virtue of the individual. The karmic justice is more exact, more immediate, and from the psychological point of view, more practical. Like the old Greek notion of cosmic justice or the traditional literary "poetic justice," karmic law demands that

---

[12] Lloyd Morris, "Anaïs Nin's Special Art," *New York Herald Tribune Book Review* (March 12, 1950), p. 17.

the punishment exactly fit the crime, that the nature of the reward proceed directly from the nature of the deed. Since to Nin morality is psychological rather than theological, the "mystical geometry" of karma, this "arithmetic of the unconscious which impelled the balancing of events" has unlimited potential as a thematic principle (*Winter*, 67).[13]

In *House of Incest* karmic justice in operation is illustrated in a number of cases. The parable of "the woman without arms" is one. "My arms were taken away from me, she sang. I was punished for clinging. I clung. . . . I wanted to caress, to heal, to rock, to lull, to surround, to encompass. And I strained and I held so much that they broke. . . . I was condemned not to hold." But then, because through the dance she comes to recognize her error, she is appropriately rewarded with their return: "she relinquished and forgave, opening her arms and her hands, permitting all things to flow away and beyond her" (*House*, 51).

In the same novel the "paralytic" acts as a variation on this theme. Like Lawrence's Clifford in *Lady Chatterley's Lover*, Anaïs Nin's paralytic is symbolic of the Hamlet-like indecision and intellectualism of modern civilization. But whereas Clifford's paralysis was only partial, this character's body is completely paralyzed. He is a novelist, and since to poetic Nin "the richest source of creation is feeling," his punishment is karmically appropriate.[14]

But the best and most original application of the theme is in her depiction of "the Modern Christ" who sits "in an agony of a secret torture." Through this modern reedemer, strikingly similar to Nathanael West's Miss Lonelyhearts, Anaïs Nin visits retributive justice upon all neurotic mankind. "Meet the Modern Christ," she writes, "who is crucified by his own nerves for all our neurotic sins!" Ironically, born without a skin, "His" greatest pain is "to be touched by a human being" (*House*, 50).

All these, however, are essentially static examples. In *Winter of Artifice* karmic justice operates dramatically in the balancing of the scales between "he" and "she." She, the narrator, is punished for making him "god the father" by eventually discovering that he is only man the child. He, on the other hand, is punished for his initial desertion of the child by being ultimately deserted by the child become woman.

There is another side to the theme of karma. Not only is karmic justice exact in the sense that it demands a precise correlation between the crime and the punishment, it is also exact in the sense that it forces the individual to reenact the pattern of sin and retribution until he comes to an

---

[13] Nin's poetic use of the idea of karma is very close to Dante's in the *Purgatorio*. But while in Dante the punishment fits the crime equally in the *Inferno*, one notices that for Nin karma is clearly purgation, and thus instead of Dante's "Abandon hope all ye who enter here," above the doorway to her cathartic chambers are inscribed hopeful words. See below, p. 97.

[14] *Realism and Reality*, p. 20.

awareness of the meaning of both. "You will never rest until you have discovered the familiar within the unfamiliar," Doctor Hernandez tells Lillian (*Seduction,* 19).

In *Seduction of the Minotaur* there are a number of such repeaters. O'Connor, the Irish archaeologist, has two obsessions: opening jail doors and searching for fragments of vanished civilizations. In the process of their conversation Lillian learns from him that during his adolescent years he had been prevented from pursuing his interests, a restriction that led to a failure of love and communication between himself and his family. Unable to accept this early emotional estrangement he turns his personal problem—the search for his lost family and the freeing of himself from its domination—into the impersonal one, but repetitive none the less, of excavating for ruins and freeing of prisoners.

But Lillian herself is the best example of the karmic repeater. The purpose of her journey to Golconda is to forget, yet little by little she reinvests her new acquaintances with old and problematic personalities. With the American prisoner and with the young student, Fred, she reenacts her initial and conscience-pricking relationship with her husband. Through the child Lietta she re-experiences her feelings about her own children and about her own childhood. With the homosexual Michael she relives the incompatibilities of her first encounter with her first anemic lover, Gerard. "We may seem to forget a person, a place, a state of being, a past life," Doctor Hernandez tells her, "but meanwhile what we are doing is selecting a new cast for the reproduction of the same drama, seeking the closest reproduction to the friend, the lover, or the husband we are trying to forget" (*Seduction,* 19).

The final aspect of the karmic doctrine that Anaïs Nin elicits, adapts, and utilizes for her own purposes is "the search for self." The motive behind the karmic repetition, behind the workings of karmic justice, is the search for knowledge of the real self, a knowledge that is possible only when the other "selves" are accepted and subsequently transcended. The parallels between such a process and the methods of psychoanalysis are obvious. But in both cases, it is as means to poetic ends, not as ends in themselves, that she finds them valuable.[15]

The search for the self may be directed inward or outward: the former usually takes the shape of the dream or reverie; the latter is conducted through the analysis of one's relationships with others.

In *House of Incest,* as the title indicates, the search is introspective. The narrator's problem is to recognize and to reconcile various inhabitants of the "house," and in doing so to transcend them, thus overcoming the nar-

---

[15] For an excellent discussion of Karma, its literary and poetic potential, see Herbert Fingarette, *The Self in Transformation* (New York, 1963).

cissistic bond that prevents her from loving *another*. "If only we could all escape from this house of incest, where we only love ourselves in the other," the Modern Christ says to her.

In "The Writer and the Symbols," Anaïs Nin explains that all her books "end with a return to the dream, not as an escape, but as a key to character. I describe many times, in various ways, the loss of the true self in relationships, and the return to the source where the genuine self lies imbedded."[16] The dream is the key to character for the dreamer also. Djuna describes the dream as "this heightened theatre" in which her life and relationships "appeared in their true color because there was no witness to distort the private admissions, the most absurd pretensions" (*Heart,* [172]). Through her long self-examination at the close of *Four-Chambered Heart,* she comes to recognize her own limitations and desires, thus achieving a certain measure of self-awareness. Through her dream she comes to see that "an individually perfect world" is impossible in reality, that her heroically proportioned mate is really only a "child lodged in a big man's body," that for her "complicity in the dark she must share the consequences." As a result she is able to *awaken* and walk *ashore.*

The outward search for self in these novels consists in the critical appraisal of the type of relationships that one forms. It is for this reason that Anaïs Nin's protagonists are provided with more than the conventional number of male companions, why they also become involved in lesbianism. In the short story, "Sabina," Djuna and Jay argue over the motives prompting the escapades of the legendary Don Juan. Djuna, speaking for her creator, says,

> "Oh, no. Don Juan was seeking in passion, in the act of possession, in the welding of bodies something that has nothing to do with passion and was never born of it."
>
> "A Narcissus pool," Jay said.
>
> "No, he was seeking to be created, to be born, to be warmed into existence, to be imagined, to be known, to be identified, he was seeking a procreative miracle. The first birth is often a failure." ("Sabina," 59)

While Djuna's analysis is, perhaps, too quixotic to be taken seriously, it does explain the karmic motive behind the erotic involvements of Nin's characters.

Sabina, the Dona Juana of *A Spy in the House of Love,* puts the theory into practice. From each of the five men she encounters she extracts one of her "selves." Her husband Alan calls her "my little one." She plays Isolde to Philip's Tristan. To Mambo she is a selfish pleasure-seeker; to the young aviator she is "a bad woman"; to Donald she is a mother and guardian. None of these selves taken separately is the real Sabina. The real heroine is the transcendental bond that links the partial

---

16 "The Writer and the Symbols," p. 59.

sketches. But to discover this transcendental self it is necessary to recognize and accept these partial manifestations—to view from a distance and objectively, the subjective. Sabina fails in her karmic search because she is not able to extract the significance of each of her encounters. She merely acts. Lillian, on the other hand, acts and analyzes. In *Ladders to Fire* she plays mother to Jay, matriarch to her husband, warrior to Gerard. In *Seduction of the Minotaur* she recognizes, accepts and then transcends these unnatural selves, and in the process discovers her real self. "One can't throw anything away forever," but one can get beyond.[17]

In "The Art of Anaïs Nin," William Burford provides an adequate explanation of the meaning of the words "creation" and "destruction" in the Nin context:

> By destruction she means a person's loss of individuality so that he or she cannot act according to feeling, intuition, desire, so that the individual lives in a state of frustration and anxiety which renders him or her incapable of happiness. By creation she means the liberation of anxiety so that achievements and desire become equivalent, so that nothing separates the two.[18]

As a result of their various experiences Anaïs Nin's characters take either of these two directions but not in the way that one usually associates with plot in the literary sense or with success or failure in a practical sense. "There is no curve nor are there any points to determine the exact course" along which her characters progress or regress. Nin wants no absolutes, "our clinging to an idea of *what should be,* rather than trying to *understand* what is" (*Lawrence,* 52). But as Burford suggests, there are certain reactions that may be considered indicative of creation or destruction.

"Tropism" is the reaction associated with creativity in the Nin world; "Tropic, from the Greek, signified change and turning" (*Seduction,* 5-6). Just as the primary characteristic of a healthy living organism is its ability to change and grow, so must the healthy psyche be able to adapt to various experiences. "Life is a process of *becoming,* a combination of states we have to go through" (*Lawrence,* 11).

Destruction, on the other hand, is the symptom and effect of fixation. "Fixation is death," says Djuna; "to be becalmed meant to die" for Sabina. And, in her "study" of Lawrence, Nin herself adds: "Where people fail is that they wish to elect a state and remain in it. That is a kind of death" (*Lawrence,* 11). In her novels, she explores a number of states in which her heroines attempt to remain. The two most obvious are the states of childhood and adolescence.

Because Nin does not follow a chronological plan of development in her novels the reader is made aware of her characters' childhood and adolescence

---

[17] Cf. *House:* "One woman within another eternally, in a far reaching procession . . . .", p. 16.

[18] Burford, p. 11.

through the flashback technique. The method has its limitations. It links the present with the past in too direct a way. Since it is usually during moments of emotional stress that her characters reminisce, the reader gets the impression that the reason for the current problem is a traumatic childhood experience. Many times this is meant to be so, but at the same time she wants the reader to realize that the reminiscence of a traumatic childhood may be an index to the speaker's present condition rather than an explanation of it. As we have seen, she uses the word "elect" rather than a deterministic term to describe the cause of fixation. Similarly, in "The Writer and the Symbols" she echoes Thomas Hardy—"Our fate is what we call our character,"—but then she adds, "The more we know about this character, the more we are able to direct our destiny and reach our fullest development."[19] Her position on child psychology, therefore, is closer to the open-ended theories of Erik Erikson than to the Freudian *cul de sac*.[20] She does not believe that there is no escape from early traumatic experiences. The individual who has suffered from an unhealthy childhood may have a more difficult time of adjusting than the normal human being, but with knowledge and determination, she believes, even the most crippling experiences can be overcome.

Each of the four main characters in her novels has had an unfortunate childhood experience. But whereas Sabina and Stella remain crippled and fixated (indicated by the unresolved endings of the novels in which they are the protagonists), Lillian and Djuna prove that the theory of "fatality" is a neurotic defense mechanism. The reason that the former pair fail, while the latter succeed, is that both Lillian and Djuna submit themselves to a rigid self-analysis (the literary equivalent to psychoanalysis), and both have the honesty to admit what they discover, and the determination to find a way of overcoming it. Sabina and Stella, on the other hand, are too self-pitying and too prone to flee from rather than to seduce the minotaur.

Through the voice of one of her characters, Anaïs Nin suggests that, like the various phases of childhood and adolescence, love also consists of a number of states that the lovers should pass through together: "Each year, just as a tree puts forth a new ring of growth, she should have been able to say: 'Alan [her husband], here is a new version of Sabina, add it to the rest, fuse them well, hold on to them when you embrace her'" (*Spy,* 59). And in her "study" of D. H. Lawrence's "Relations between men and women" Nin writes: "In marriage, more than in any other relationship, the question of oscillation is . . . crucial. Over a certain number of years people undergo changes of many kinds, but because at a certain moment

---

[19] "The Writer and the Symbols," pp. 38-39.
[20] For Erikson's disagreement with Freud see especially "Childhood and the Modalities of Social Life," Part I of *Childhood and Society,* Second Edition (New York, 1963), pp. 21-108.

two individuals stood together on the same peak, we mistakenly believe they can always grow in the same direction" (*Lawrence*, 59). The question of constancy and change in love is a key theme in her own work also and indicates her affinity to the English artist. Lawrence tried to solve the problem of marriage by suggesting a relationship based on the admission of two integrities, each recognizing the ultimate independence of the other. Nin is less dogmatic than Lawrence, more concerned with the reasons for incompatibility than with the solution, and more willing to put the blame and the responsibility on the individual himself rather than on the institution.

In *Seduction of the Minotaur* she explains that there is one basic barrier to a healthy and productive relationship: the *myth,* both the "self-created myth" which the individual wraps himself in as a protection against reality, and the myth created by others, which is a projection of their own need. Lillian's private myth portrayed her as an aggressive, love-lavishing woman; her husband felt he needed such an Amazon to cover his own reticencies. But actually, it is Lillian who needs to be the loved one, just as Djuna needs to be recognized, not as the angelic creature that everyone thinks she is, but as the sensual woman she latently is. Because both these heroines come to an awareness of the falsity of the roles that they themselves and others have forced upon them, and because both are determined to stop such posturing, they are permitted to "come up" from the "cities of the interior." Djuna is able to laugh at "the doll that committed suicide during the night" (*Heart,* [178]), and Lillian is able to journey homeward.

The final state that must be experienced but which must never be allowed to become a resting place is the dream. The dream can be either an escape or "the seed for the miracle and the fulfillment" (*Bell,* 15). Like all transcendentalists, Anaïs Nin looks at the phenomenal world as the dressing of reality. In the dream one comes into direct contact with "the real"; hence its importance: "The greatest of all joys is to be able to retrace one's lies, to return to the source and sleep one night a year washed of all superstructures" (*House,* 20). But to persist in the dream state is as bad as not to dream at all: "We cannot stay at the source all the time." In her short stories, "Je suis le plus malade des surrealistes," "The Eye's Journey," and "Under a Glass Bell," she dramatically illustrates what happens to those who remain in "the somnambulistic garden": all the characters in these stories are eventually revealed to be insane.

Karma, Tropism, and Fixation, then, are the three controlling ideas in the Nin novels. Because they are basic rather than individualized themes, in the preceding pages they have been illustrated with examples chosen at random from all of her works. It will now be interesting and helpful to examine the development of these themes in her portrayal of a specific character and the series of novels in which she appears. The progress of Djuna is well suited for such purposes.

The theme of the first novel in which Djuna appears—*Winter of Artifice,* Part I—is a variation of the fixation motif. In the opening passages of this work, the heroine is described as awaiting the arrival of a male figure identified only as "he." The technique is very subtle, for the narrator's intimate tone and the fact that Djuna has been waiting for twenty years for "him" lead the reader to anticipate a reunion of lovers. The symbolism of the "glass bowl with the glass fish and the glass ship," however, indicates that whatever the nature of the reunion there is something definitely unnatural about it.

Instead of enlarging upon Djuna's problem in a direct manner, the narrator lapses into a lengthy reverie. In the first part of this reminiscence, the narrator describes Djuna's early childhood, and the reader learns that the most significant incident in the heroine's life, and the one from which she has not recovered, is her father's desertion of her when she was a child of nine. "Since that day she had not seen her father. Twenty years have passed. He is coming today. She is thirty years old . . ." (*Winter*, 7).

Having located the cause of Djuna's fixation, the narrator goes on to describe the kind of activity Djuna has engaged in as a result of this experience: "little by little, she shut herself up within the walls of her diary," and more and more she has withdrawn into the world of the dream. Through both these escape mechanisms, "she created another world," and thus the reader is forewarned that the awaited personage has, in Djuna's mind, been exaggerated out of all proportion, and that for her he is no longer merely a man but the hero of her individual myth.

The father arrives—in appearance the fulfillment of all her expectations. But unfortunately, "His face wore a mask." Despite her intellectual awareness that the appearance may be deceiving, however, Djuna's childish need allows her to overlook the possible discrepancies between the mask and the man behind it. "She forgot for the moment everything she knew, surrendered her own certainties" (*Winter*, 34). And feeling that she has reached her port at last, Djuna deliberately (the knowing reader would say "prematurely") breaks the glass bowl.

For a short while actor and actress are content to play the roles prescribed by Djuna's dream-fabricated script. He poses as "the father, the seer, the god"; she plays the devoted daughter, the worshipful disciple, the adoring goddess. They spend their time delighting in what appear to be their remarkable similarities: "Echoes. Echoes. Blood echoes. Yes, yes to everything. Exactly. She knew it. That is what she hoped. The same: father and daughter. Unison. The same rhythm" (*Winter*, 23). Their relationship, obviously, is not as incestuous as it is narcissistic. Each loves the self in the other.

In accordance with the karmic idea of exact punishment, this selfishness that originally brought them together and upon which they established their relationship now begins to force them apart. He becomes obsessed with jealousy because he finds that she is not completely his "double"—she is capable of having interests other than those they share. She becomes filled with disgust because of the lies she is forced to tell to satisfy his egotism, and because she finally realizes that his entire life has been a pattern of lies. "This was the winter of artifice."

Djuna's awareness that this performance must now come to an end is precipitated by two things. First, her father is stricken with a case of lumbago, which she describes as symbolic of "the stiffness in the joints of his soul, from acting and pretending." Second, the father "abdicates" his role as protector and ruler by calling her "an Amazon," a woman, as Djuna reasons, who "does not need a father. Nor a lover nor a husband" (*Winter*, 35). An Amazon does not need love—she gives it; an Amazon does not need protection—she protects. As the implications of these two incidents become obvious to Djuna, "the cold, white fog of falsity" begins to rise. She realizes that her father always was and always will be a child. At the same time she recognizes her own childish refusal to recognize this fact even when confronted with evidence.

When her father was leaving the house the day he deserted her, she had clung to his coat. "*Today she held the coat of a dead love*. This had been the nightmare—to pursue this search and poison all joys with the necessity of its fulfillment. To discover that such fulfillment was not necessary to life, but to the myth" (*Winter*, 83). Finally shaking off her childish fixation, Djuna comes "out of the ether of the past."

In Part II of *Winter of Artifice*, Djuna is portrayed in another stage of her development, and illustrates another of the basic Nin themes. Her problem is to find a way of accepting the flow of life and the eternal metamorphosis that is characteristic of it without becoming submerged and stripped of her identity by it.

The opening paragraph of the novel introduces this theme in the symbolism of the "cell-shaped room" in "the tallest hotel of the city." In the room lies Djuna, alone, inert, and in a state of reverie; outside the room, the hotel elevators rush up and down like "great swooping birds"; the "singing, the weeping, the quarrels and confessions" seep down the halls in a Babel-like confusion. Doors are banging, the chambermaid is passing, the messenger boy is running, the house detective is watching. To find some way of fusing these two modes of existence—the isolated dream state on the one hand, the confused waking state on the other—is Djuna's problem, and the one that brings her to the room of the "voice."

In a series of interviews with this "substitute for God, for the confessor of old," Djuna explains that all she sees in the external world is a current of "debris"; "I seem to be standing and watching this current passing and I am left behind." To this the voice replies, "Only because you are standing still. . . . When you are living you seek the change; it is only when you stop that you become aware of death" (*Winter*, 89). For the moment the answer is sufficient. Djuna leaves her cell-shaped room and allows herself to be caught up in the "street eddies" of the outside world.

When she returns to the hotel, however, she finds the lobby filled with people from her past. She is startled and frightened: "Surely she had thrown them out with the broken toys, but they sat there, threatening to sweep her back. . . . Could all escape be an illusion?" she finally asks, and thus informs the reader that her surrender to the flow of the outside world had been motivated, not by a desire to become a positive, active part of the collective life, but by a desire to escape in a negative passive way from the burdens of the past.

Unaware that "nothing can be thrown away forever," Djuna seeks absolution in the ritual of washing her hair: "The water runs softly through the roots of the being, like warm rain, and washes away everything" (*Winter*, 105). But of course when she returns, the ghosts of the past are still seated in the lobby. According to the karmic scheme, absolution is not granted, it is earned.

Djuna is about to despair when she hears "a dull powerful sound outside. A heavy sound but dull, without an echo. . . . A woman had thrown herself from a window. . . . She was dead, of course, dead with a five month old child inside her" (*Winter*, 106). The woman's suicide—caused by loneliness—with life inside her yet afraid to face the life outside—parallels Djuna's despair and her attempt to drown herself in the flow of the external world. If the dead woman had been able to communicate with another, she would not have despaired; she could have faced the life outside and given birth to the new life within.

Aware of these implications and profiting from them, Djuna begins to come out of the world of the dream, begins to consciously seek out others and their problems. When she returns to the room of the voice, the roles are curiously reversed. She becomes the one who listens and sympathizes. And out in the streets "she felt the multiple footsteps of those walking along with her, not like a march, but like a symphony. In the shock of feet against the pavements she felt the whole collision and impact of human being against human being" (*Winter*, 129). With nature also, she now feels in harmony: "Djuna was one with the moon."

Djuna's new awareness that it is possible to be separate and related simultaneously is symbolized by her relationship with Lilith. As the name indicates, Lilith is a seducer, on the one hand, and a "woman whom man cannot possess altogether," on the other (*Winter*, 139). Through her "communion" with Lilith, Djuna loses her separate identity. Yet because Lilith cannot be possessed by man, Djuna-Lilith retains her separateness.

But while Djuna now has the theoretical solution to her problem, the dream still has too great a power over her to allow her to perfectly practice her theories. Thus the novel closes with the simple sentence: "Awareness hurts" followed by a lengthy dream monologue.

In *Four-Chambered Heart,* Djuna resumes the familiar conflict between the external and dream worlds, but in this case the theme is presented in terms of an orthodox sexual relationship, and in this novel the heroine finally does free herself from all the various aspects of her neurosis.

When Djuna first meets Rango, "the idol of the night clubs," she thinks he is a gypsy, "A man who had never been bound" (*Heart* [3]). Selecting him as the one to lead her to "the unattainable island of joy" she had once visited in a dream, she coquettishly asks him to play for her dancing. And he agrees.

However, as they plan their future encounter, Djuna discovers that not only is he not a gypsy, but he is forced to spend the greater part of his life in a "gray stone house" caring for a sick wife. Pitying him, and determined to have her dream realized despite all odds, Djuna rents a houseboat—a meeting place removed from the oppressing realities of life on the shore.

As is usual in the case of such a dream-relationship, each character assumes the role that the other expects of him: Rango sees Djuna as an angel of mercy, her "good self" only; Djuna, on the other hand, wants a legendary hero, and thus sees Rango as the epitome of strength and wisdom. During the brief time that each party is content to play the appointed role, they "reached a perfect moment of human love."

But soon the roles begin to cramp: Djuna starts to rebel against the appeal only to her "good self"; she discovers that her lover is only a big child. From the shore, the demands of Zora, Rango's wife, and the Revolution begin to destroy the dream life on the barge.

Unable to face the destruction of her dream, but also realizing that the "barge was sailing nowhere," Djuna decides to sink the craft, and she and her lover with it. But as she lies beside him "to wait patiently for death," she begins a long and rigorous self-examination. During the course of her reverie she comes to realize that the reason for her suicidal gesture is that she "was ashamed of this shrinking and fading, of what time would do to our fiction of magnificence" (*Heart,* [173]). She forces herself to admit that she is making a "selfish" and a pointless journey, that there is no island of complete joy, no individually perfect world. Not change, but fixation brings death. "The trap was the static pause in growth, the arrested self caught in its own web of obstinacy and obsession. . . ." Not only aware now that tropism and realism are essential to life, but determined also to give both change and the dream their proper emphasis, Djuna wakes her lover and walks ashore. "Noah's ark had survived the flood" (*Heart,* [178]).

It should now be obvious that, if Anaïs Nin's themes owe much to the discoveries and theories of psychoanalysis, her development of them is not clinical but artistic. This point cannot be overemphasized. Of course Nin, herself, is partially responsible for this need of exaggerated emphasis through her fondness for psychoanalytic terminology; though one must admit that she never uses a clinical term without giving it artistic connotations, and that she almost completely confines her faddishness to her critical writing. In her fiction, symbolism, myth, and poetic prose transform what may have been a case-study into a perceptive and aesthetically satisfying work of art.

"Many novels today include the psychoanalytic experience," she writes, but "that is only a crude makeshift."[21] It is not the methods and techniques of the psychoanalyst that must be adopted as "an integral part of the novelist's equipment." It is the power, the insight, and the knowledge of the science that is valuable to the writer. Psychoanalysis is a source for the artist, not a means or end in itself. In short, *Four-Chambered Heart* is a poetic novel, not a medical report.

---

[21] *Realism and Reality*, p. 19.

IV

☆ ☆ ☆ ☆ ☆

An Edifice Without Dimension

In his review of the first volume of Nin's *Diary*, Karl Shapiro implies that the only possible critical study of the Nin novels is a study of their genesis:

> These works are, even on the authority of Miss Nin, distillations from the 150 volumes or so of the *Diary*. They are, so to speak, the *Diary* writing poems. Undoubtedly one of the reasons why her novels have not been properly valued is the unavailability of the main work. Without the masterpiece of the journal the novels remain shadowy, obscure, beautiful fragments.[1]

While Shapiro's desire to explain Anaïs Nin's lack of popularity is understandable, his method of doing so is both unfortunate and unsound. Unfortunate, because the priority of the *Diary* has become a *donnée* in studies of her art: "Any discussion of Anaïs Nin's work must properly begin with her *Diary*, for from the first it has been the source of all her fiction,"[2] announces a recent critic unequivocally at the beginning of his study. Unsound, because not only have Nin's comments on the matter been accepted as the final word but they have also been awkwardly interpreted. Significantly, Shapiro's authority for his observation is Gunther Stuhlmann, the editor of the *Diary*: "Anaïs Nin herself has often stated that the body of her published, artistic work—the five novels which make up the *roman fleuve, Cities of the Interior,* and her other books and stories—were merely outcroppings of the diary, and that her real life, as a writer and a woman, was contained in the pages of the journal." But "merely outcroppings" is scarcely the impression created by the quotation he uses to support this observation: " 'I have a natural flow in the diary,' she wrote more than thirty years ago, 'what I produce outside is a distillation, the myth, the poem.' "[3] Instead of a dismissal of the fiction the passage clearly is concerned with establishing a contrast between two kinds of art, between the spontaneous fluidity of the journal and (in contrast) the conscious formalism of the fiction. The passage does not assign greater literary value to the *Diary;* indeed, if anything should suggest the autonomy and artistry of the fiction it is the words "produce," "myth," and "poem." Even in a literal sense, furthermore, "distillation" implies essence, the most valuable, rather than excerpt or fragment. Finally,

---

[1] Karl Shapiro, "The Charmed Circle of Anaïs Nin," *Book Week* (May 1, 1966), p. 3.
[2] Evans, *Anaïs Nin*, p. 3.
[3] Gunther Stuhlmann, "Introduction," *The Diary of Anaïs Nin: 1931–1934* (New York, 1966), p. v.

if the *Diary* is an artistic work, then a certain amount of circumspection must be exercised in quoting from it. For even if Stuhlmann's interpretation were accurate, one would still have to take into account what Nin says elsewhere on the subject.

In *On Writing,* for example, she describes the *Diary* as a workshop in which she prepares for the writing of the fiction:

> Keeping a Diary all my life helped me to discover some basic elements essential to the vitality of writing. . . . Improvisation, free association, obedience to mood, impulse, brought forth countless images, portraits, descriptions, impressionistic sketches, symphonic experiments from which I could dip at any time for material. . . . Sheer playing of scales, practice, repetition—then by the time one is ready to write a story or novel a great deal of natural distillation and softening has been accomplished.[4]

The impression created here is almost directly opposite to that which Stuhlmann describes; here the *Diary* is given secondary and the fiction primary importance. But the passage is valuable essentially as a corrective. Considered objectively, the best analogue for Nin's practice is that of Emerson and Thoreau, both of whom wrote lengthy private journals which functioned as the source for their public art. One would not think of calling Emerson's essays or Thoreau's *Walden* "merely outcroppings"; that Anaïs Nin's *Diary* provides the seminal context for her fiction and that it is important in itself as a literary creation similarly should not relegate the fiction to second place.

In the early stages of her career, one might also recall, Nin herself had numerous quarrels with her associates concerning the relationship between the *Diary* and the fiction. Henry Miller wanted her to elaborate in the novels as she did in the *Diary;* Otto Rank wanted her to use the *Diary* merely as a sketchbook. Though occasionally she admitted that there was some wisdom in their words, she more often felt that both Rank and Miller misunderstood the nature of her fiction and that it was this that made them criticize the *Diary.* They wanted her to write novels with elaborate and explicit characterization and incident; she wanted to "write as a poet in the framework of prose."[5] And this leads us back to the present. For while part of the misunderstanding concerning the nature of the novels results from a confusion of the historical and literary priority of the *Diary,* a great part results from a failure on the part of critics and reviewers to understand the experimental nature of her work. An examination of the form of the Nin novels should clarify both types of misunderstanding.

Again it is a matter of "realism and reality." In his "Studies in the Contemporary Novel," Ihab Hassan defines form as "the way the mind acknowledges experience. It is a mode of awareness."[6] The form of the

---

[4] *On Writing,* p. 21.

[5] *Realism and Reality,* p. 13.

[6] Ihab Hassan, *Radical Innocence: Studies in the Contemporary American Novel* (Princeton, 1961), p. 99.

traditional novel is a reflection of an empirical and historical mode of perception. Fielding and Defoe are only the technical parents of the genre; philosophically, as Philip Stevick suggests, "Since Ian Watt's *The Rise of the Novel,* it has become customary to speak of the novel as the product of an intellectual milieu shaped by Descartes and Locke. It is a milieu which contains an insistence upon the importance of individual experience, a distrust of universals, and an elevation of the senses as the necessary means by which ideas are formed."[7] The chronological narrative pattern of such fiction thus is not the invention of a single mind but the reflection of the age and its adherence to a linear and historical concept of time; the chapter method and the logical development of theme reflect a scientific and materialistic attitude toward experience. "One reflects," continues Stevick, "on how long narrative literature was able to get along without representing the minute passage of time, precisely located space, and carefully observed appearances and one concludes that novels represent these aspects of experience not because novelists developed a superior degree of skill but because a particular philosophical climate had made it legitimate to think of sensory data and individual experience as the very substance of reality itself."

Nin's "philosophical climate" is radically different from that of the eighteenth-century, and for this reason she demands new forms for fiction. Her mode of awareness is psychological and transcendental. The unconscious and the transcendental are timeless dimensions; instinct has nothing to do with external appearances and intuition is by definition a-logical. It is not the individual experience but the subjectivity of experience that engages her. The form of her fiction, in short, reflects a milieu shaped by Emerson and Cassirer and Freud and Rank. With Virginia Woolf, she asks the paired questions: "Is life like this? Must novels be like this?"

In addition to this general philosophical reason for a change in the form of the novel, Nin specifically adds a cultural argument. "The conventionalities of the novel can no longer communicate what we know," she states in *On Writing,* and by "what we know" she refers to the "new dimension," "the unconscious."[8] Novelists of previous times, she is aware, have known about this dimension and have recognized its importance in character development, but they called it motivation and presented its operations implicitly. The reason that the modern writer cannot be content with such a method is not simply that he technically knows more about the workings of the unconscious but rather that the modern world has become increasingly neurotic and consequently in need of more explicit analysis. "The novelist knows that psychoanalysis has uncovered layers not uncovered in the narrative novel (particularly in a society where people's acts no longer correspond to

[7] Philip Stevick, "Introduction" to *The Theory of the Novel* (New York, 1967), pp. 6-7.
[8] *Realism and Reality,* p. 17.

their inner impulses . . . ."[9] It is as much because today we rationalize too much and feel too little as that we made advances in psychology that the novelist should explicitly avail himself of psychoanalytic techniques. When man acted according to his impulses the unconscious could be rendered implicitly through narrative; but this is not the shape of life today, and consequently neither is the conventional narrative an adequate form of fiction.

Nin's definition of the appropriate form for the novel and thus an index to the narrative mode of fiction may be found in the foreword to her earliest work, *House of Incest:* "All that I know is contained in this book written without witness, an edifice without dimension, a city hanging in the sky."

As the "I" indicates, in the first place, all of Nin's fiction is structured upon the principle of limited point of view. In *House of Incest* she employs a first person narrator; in the succeeding novels she uses the third person narrative mode, but she continues to limit the perspective to the main character. Lillian, Djuna, Stella, and Sabina are, as one critic aptly describes them, "sensitive registers,"[10] or as James would say, "vessels of consciousness." And in the best Jamesian manner Nin's characters are depicted through their musings rather than through authorial comment. On the other hand, whereas even in his most "limited" fictions James always includes a plot, the entire narrative of a Nin novel is, as Harriet Zinnes suggests, "a long monologue of a self revealed";[11] and whereas James' work is characterized by the irony resulting from the narrator's limited consciousness, Nin's work is characterized by a tension in the narrator herself.

A clue to the special type of narration used by Nin is to be found in her attempt to define the type of language Lawrence uses in his symbolic passages: "A great part of his writing might be called 'interlinear' because of his constant effort to make conscious and articulate the silent subconscious communications between human beings" (*Lawrence,* 6). The vantage point from which the Nin narrator tells her story is also "interlinear," between the "cold grey upper leaf of dawn [the conscious], or the dark layer of night [the unconscious]." Situated on this level she is able, like the day-dreamer, to be both a participator in and a spectator of her own drama. In *Realism and Reality* she explains that the motive behind this technique is "to poetize and analyze simultaneously."[12] Thus Nin's narrative voice is really a duet, the product of the tension between two modes of apprehension. In the Stella portion of *Ladders to Fire* a musical analogy is used to dramatize the conflicting feelings in the heroine. The passage applies equally well to the use of a vocal duet as a narrative technique:

---

[9] *Ibid.,* p. 18.
[10] Morris, p. 17.
[11] Harriet Zinnes, "Anaïs Nin's Works Reissued," *Books Abroad,* XXXVII, (1963), p. 284.
[12] *Realism and Reality,* p. 14.

In music there was a parallel to the conflict which disturbed her. Within
the concerto too the feminine and the masculine elements were inter-
acting. The trombone, with its assertions, and the flute, with its sinuosities. . . .

And as for the flute, it was so easily victimized and overpowered. But
it triumphed ultimately because it left an echo. Long after the trombone
had had its say, the flute continued its mischievous, insistent tremolos.
(*Ladders*, 17)

The assertive voice of the trombone represents the analysing voice of the
consciousness; the sinuosities of the flute correspond to the unverbalized
emotions. In "Anaïs Nin's Special Art" Lloyd Morris explains why such a
technique is required: "For Miss Nin is not, in the usual sense, trying to tell
a story. Her object is to reveal experience directly. She wishes to immerse
readers in that flow of sensibility and reflection from which human beings
distill the significance of what they do and suffer."[13] Whereas the traditional
novel is concerned with doing and reflection and stream-of-consciousness
fiction is concerned with sensibility and suffering, Nin attempts to present
both, simultaneously.

"Written without witness" is the second part of Nin's definition, and this
phrase provides the second clue to the peculiar form to be found in her
novels. In the context of her conflict with the realists, "witness" refers to the
objective author, the detached commentator who strives to remain aloof
from the experience to be communicated. "Written without witness," then,
refers to Anaïs Nin's opposite method and indicates at once the subjectivity
that is characteristic of her writing. In *On Writing* she attempts to anticipate
the objections of those who make distance the *sine qua non* of art: "This
personal relationship to all things, which is condemned as subjective, limiting, I found to be the core of individuality, personality and originality. The
idea that subjectivity is an impasse is as false as the idea that objectivity
leads to a larger form of life."[14] But this does not mean that Nin is writing
"fictionalized autobiography," or that "one is morally blackmailed at the
start, since, by this entangling alliance, strictly *literary* criticism is almost
proscribed."[15] In his study, *The Modern Psychological Novel*, Leon Edel
makes the observation "that whereas all artists utilize personal experience, in
the psychological novel the traditional process of projecting the inner experience into an imaginative narrative dealing with the external world was not
carried out. These novelists sought to retain and record the 'inwardness' of
experience."[16] It is in this tradition that Nin belongs and it is because of
this that she describes her novels as "dramas as the unconscious lives them."[17]

[13] Morris, p. 17.
[14] *On Writing*, p. 22.
[15] Vernon Young, p. 427.
[16] Leon Edel, *The Modern Psychological Novel* (New York, 1964), p. 12.
[17] *Realism and Reality*, p. 14.

The locale of the Nin novels, then, is not the phenomenal but the noumenal world, a world which she describes as "almost in opposition to our surface world. It is first of all ruled by flow."[18] To retain this sense of flow is the most basic of Nin's structural concerns. One of the ways she accomplishes it—Proust's way—is to make emotion and memory the determining principles of her selection and positioning of episodes and paragraphs. For example, in *Ladders to Fire,* Lillian's unsatisfactory teenage sexual encounter should chronologically be the first episode in the novel. Instead, it appears at the high point of the heroine's sexual frustration—near the middle of the novel. In *Seduction of the Minotaur,* Lillian's feelings toward a child she sees on a bus trip introduce her mental voyage back to her own childhood. Another way in which Nin baptizes her episodes in "the holy waters of continuity" is by avoiding end-stop passages. Mechanically, this means the use of elliptical marks at the end of paragraphs and sections: "It was her piano Jay had left out in the rain to be ruined . . ." (*Ladders,* 127); "Other Gerards will appear, until . . ." (74). Questions instead of affirmative statements have a similar function: "How could joy have vanished with the father?" (63); "Will you be here tomorrow, Rango?" (*Heart* [2]). Short phrases to introduce or conclude a paragraph create the impression of inconclusiveness, and thus also contribute to the impression of "a tale without beginning or end which encloses all things and relates all things."[19]

"Now I place you in a world which is like the world of the dream," Nin writes, "and I expect people to recognize its contours or its lack of contours."[20] As Joyce and Faulkner, the surrealists and the psychologists have shown, the spatial and temporal dimensions of this world are not chartable in terms of yardsticks and clocks. Since the structure of the traditional novel is based upon such phenomenal measurements, a novelist dealing with a world in which they are secondary, if relevant at all, must consequently reject the old forms patterned on them. Thus Nin's "freewheeling disregard for the conventionalities of the novel" is a purposeful rebellion rather than a destructive iconoclasm. As she explains in *On Writing:*

> Like the modern physicist the novelist of today should face the fact that this new psychological reality can be explored and dealt with only under conditions of tremendously high atmospheric pressures, temperatures and speed, as well as in terms of new time-space dimensions for which the old containers represented by the traditional forms and conventions of the novel are completely inadequate and inappropriate.[21]

---

18 "The Writer and the Symbols," p. 39.
19 *On Writing,* pp. 21-22.
20 *Realism and Reality,* p. 16.
21 *On Writing,* p. 19.

But lack of mechanical and conventional form does not necessitate formlessness. "An edifice without dimension" has its own architectural principles.

The first of these is organic development, "form created by the meaning," "born of theme."[22] In all of Nin's novels "the self [is seen] as centre of an epical event."[23] And since "the epical event" is always a search for some aspect of the self, the form imposed by the theme is usually that of a journey. In *Seduction of the Minotaur,* this theme of search and the consequent voyage-form of the novel are symbolically outlined in the opening paragraph:

> Some voyages have their inception in the blueprint of a dream, some in the urgency of contradicting a dream. Lillian's recurrent dream of a ship that could not reach water, that sailed laboriously, pushed by her with great effort, through city streets, had determined her course toward the sea, as if she would give this ship, once and for all, its proper sea bed. (*Seduction,* 5)

As her dream implies, Lillian is searching for her inner, most basic self. Hence, the journey must be to an equatorial climate. Psychologically and geographically, she must travel inward. Because the self for which she is searching has been lost in the "city streets,"—in the confusions and conventions of modern civilization—she must go to a place where the patterns of civilized behavior are not required. In short, she must go to a primitive southern village. Thus the basic structure of *Seduction of the Minotaur* is Lillian's journey to and from the Mexican city of Golconda.

In *Four-Chambered Heart* the underlying structure is similarly developed from the theme, and thus this novel also takes the form of a voyage. The heroine, Djuna, is attempting to find "an individually perfect world." Aware that such a place does not exist on *land,* she cuts herself off from the real world by going to live on a river barge. When she discovers that even in the dream (the barge) her search is futile, that is, when she reaches the port of self-awareness, she leaves the craft and comes back to shore.

In "Fiction and the 'Analogical Matrix'," Mark Schorer suggests that "metaphorical language . . . can be in novels as in poems the basis of structure."[24] Nin is of a similar opinion, and frequently makes use of this device to create order in her novels. In *Winter of Artifice,* Part I, for example, the central idea of the falsity of external appearances is presented through a series of images taken from the theatre. Djuna and her father play "roles." In her diary she creates "her double." Her father wears "a mask." When they cannot communicate they are described as "gesticulating in space." The novel closes with the following extended metaphor: "At last she was entering the Chinese theatre of her drama and could see the trappings of the play as

---

22 *Ibid.,* p. 27.

23 Paul Rosenteld, "Refinements of a Journal," *Nation* (September 26, 1942), p. 269.

24 Mark Schorer, "Fiction and the 'Analogical Matrix'," in *Critiques and Essays on Modern Fiction,* p. 98.

well as the play itself, see that the settings were made of the cardboard of illusion. She was passing behind the stage. . . . She could see the strings which ruled the scenes, the false storms and the false lightning" (*Winter*, 83).

Writing in the *Partisan Review*, Steven Marcus observes that "the governing tendency in the novel in the last fifteen or twenty years has, I think, been in the direction of poetry . . . a poetic conception both of experience and of the shapes which experience must take."[25] The characteristics of this new poeticized novel are, as he suggests, a reduction in size, dramatic rendering of theme through form, and a disciplined effort of compression. The writing of Anaïs Nin fulfills all of these qualifications. "The accelerated rhythm of modern life could not be without its counterpart in literature," she writes, "the true meaning, the true purpose of abstraction is not a dehydration of experience, but an extracting and distilling of its essence to achieve greater intensity."[26] And since she believes that it is in "the moments of emotional crises that human beings reveal themselves most accurately," her practice is to delete all prefatory and post-climactic material. For example, Sabina is introduced and described; meets, seduces and leaves five lovers; makes innumerable dream excursions; and comments on her problems, all in one hundred and thirty-six pages. Such a practice obviously does not make for lifelikeness in the documentary manner of the "realists," but because of her use of a limited point of view and the interior monologue she is able to make this "montage" of intensities emotionally convincing.

Another way in which she is able to achieve the desired condensation is to make every concrete object a symbolic one: "I never include the concrete object or fact unless it has a symbolic role to play."[27] By using this device she is able to concentrate on the significance of her drama without becoming abstract. Thus the barge on which Rango and Djuna live is also a "Noah's Ark," the River Seine is both the river—the flow of the unconscious—and a French landmark; the policeman on the shore is also Djuna's conventional conscience. It is this method, as Harriet Zinnes explains, that makes the pattern of the Nin novels poetic rather than psychoanalytic, that allows her to employ "metaphor and image to form a complex of experience unanalyzed and intact to achieve a poetic effect."[28]

There is another way in which Nin uses the symbol as a formal principle. All of her novels have symbolic titles and in each the title is the controlling idea of the material that follows. In *House of Incest*, for example, "house" is a metaphor for the body or psyche; "incest" refers to the narcissistic nature of that psyche. Similar to Melville's "Doubloon" or to Virginia Woolf's

[25] Steven Marcus, "The Novel Again," *Partisan Review*, XXIX (1962), pp. 172-173.
[26] "The Writer and the Symbols," p. 34.
[27] *Realism and Reality*, p. 14.
[28] Zinnes, pp. 283-286.

"Lighthouse" is "The Cafe," the title of a section in *Children of the Alba-tross*. The personalities of the various frequenters of the Cafe are defined in terms of its significance for them, while at the same time it functions as a structurally unifying device by bringing them all together.

Frequently Nin introduces the controlling symbol in a short introductory passage, devoting the rest of the novel to an explication of its significance in terms of the particular narrator. For example, "Stella" begins with the image of the heroine sitting "in a small, dark room" watching "her own figure acting on the screen." The "small dark room" symbolizes her introversion, the "screen" her social mask. "The obvious difference between her daily self to which she purposely brought no enhancement and the screen image which was illuminated," is the theme that the two symbols introduce (*Ladders*, 15). Similar is the opening of the Second Part of *Winter of Artifice*. In the first paragraphs Djuna is described as "lying down in a cell-shaped room of the tallest hotel in the City," a building with "a million rooms like cells," in which "the rapid birds of elevators traverse the layers with lightning flashes of their red and white eyes signalling UP or DOWN" (*Winter*, 85). The hubbub of the hotel, its height and the shape of its rooms shadow forth the neurotic conflicts and nervous strain that bring Djuna and the other characters to the room of the "voice."

In "The Writer and the Symbols" Nin describes her method of compo-sition as being partly "musical." At times this merely means that she will introduce the title of a song or concerto to provide a background for action taking place, as when Sabina "listens" to Debussy's *Ile Joyeuse* and *Clair de Lune* in her dream of "the more luminous life awaiting her." Or it may mean that a musical analogue will define the relationship between two characters, as in the "orchestral passage" in *Winter of Artifice*. Or yet again, it may mean that she will attempt to capture the rise and fall of the emo-tions by the use of carefully structured paragraphs, as in the lyrical *House of Incest*. But the way that music makes its greatest contribution to her fiction is in a type of "symphonic structure" that she uses to capture both the "cadences of a mood" and the flow of the narrator's voice.[29] Instead of "parts" and "Chapters" it is better to speak of "movements" in her novels. In *Seduction of the Minotaur* the progress and the voice of the narrator flows out in a gradually increasing crescendo in the first, or "Solar Barque," section coming to a full diapason with the death of Dr. Hernandez. Then "Lillian

---

[29] In reply to Wyndham Lewis' complaint that the stream-of-consciousness writer "robs work of all linear properties whatsoever, of all contour and definition . . . the romantic ab-dominal *within* method results in a jellyfish structure, without articulation of any sort," Leon Edel, in *The Modern Psychological Novel*, writes: "This judgment takes stock of the intellectual rather than the emotional content of the conscious," (p. 91). Edel then suggests that "There is a thematic structure one might describe as *symphonic*, which provides distinct "linear proper-ties" over and above the Homeric Frame." (italics mine)

turned and changed . . . as the jazz players swung into their rhythms, as
the sea swung in its bed

turned

changed

Lillian was journeying homeward" (*Seduction,* 95). In the remaining part
of the novel the range of the narrator's voice slowly decreases as the implications of the heroine's experience are narrowed into a focus on her
immediate situation, a hitherto unsuccessful marriage.

Despite her disregard for mechanical form, then, Nin's "edifices without
dimension" are not formless. Symbols, musical patterning and poetic devices
of organization take the place of chapters and plot in her "flowing inner
chronicle."[30] Since these new methods had, before Nin began writing, been
adopted and perfected in the "stream-of-consciousness" school, her work
though original, is not radical.

In order to provide the reader with a broad working knowledge of Nin's
method of assembling and organizing her material, it has been necessary to
deal with her techniques in a comprehensive way and to use a wide variety
of examples. It is now interesting and enlightening to examine the way in
which the various devices are used in the construction of a single work.

A Spy in the House of Love is both a delightful manual of love's subter-
fuges, and a psychologically perceptive study of a woman's passions. The
theme of this novel is a variant of the Lawrence "separateness-relatedness"
idea—the need for stability in love counterpointed by the need for mobility.
The heroine, Sabina, like all of Nin's heroines is a composite of various
selves: "not ONE, but a multitude of Sabinas" (*Spy,* 105). Unfortunately her
husband, Alan, is capable of recognizing and appreciating only the "little
girl" Sabina he had married some years earlier. Sabina, consequently, feels
forced to go out to find mates for the other facets of her personality.

The basic structure "born of this theme" is best suggested by a geo-
metrical image: the compass. The fixed foot corresponds to the need for
stability and is represented by Sabina's husband and home, a point to which
she always returns after her various escapades. The free foot traces the
various paths that Sabina takes to satisfy her need for mobility.

At the same time the novel also has a type of linear structure arising from
the secondary theme, the conflict between temperament and conscience. At
the beginning of the novel, a mysterious character called the "lie detector"
is introduced and announces his intention of following Sabina. Though after
his initial appearance in the bar he drops out of sight and does not appear
again until the end of the novel, Sabina's tortured awareness that she is
being followed makes him a valuable connecting link between the various
episodes.

---

[30] William Goyen, "Bits and Images of Life," *New York Herald Tribune Book Review*
(November 29, 1964), p. 5.

A third way in which Nin is able to provide unity and continuity without the imposition of mechanical form is through the use of carefully chosen imagistic and metaphoric patterns. Derived from the mobility aspect of her theme are a group of images associated with transportation. Sabina, herself, is described as evoking "the sound and imagery of fire engines as they tore through the streets." Similarly, the cape that she always wears and flings over her shoulder as she is about to set out on one of her excursions creates the impression of flight and swiftness.

Three of Sabina's sexual encounters are directly associated with modes of transportation. She and Philip enjoy their first intimate relationship at the bottom of a sailboat. She first meets John, an aviator, and the third of her lovers, when he comes to a stop on his bicycle at an intersection. Because they had "no place to go," Sabina recalls, she and Jay satisfied their erotic desires in a rapidly ascending and descending elevator. Red and green traffic lights, buses, trucks, streets, roads, and alleys also play their part in creating an atmosphere of flight and mobility, and in linking each of the episodes to the theme.

In contrast to these images are those related to the other aspect of the theme—the need for stability. Alan, Sabina's husband, appears as "a fixed point in space. A calm face. A calm bearing." When Sabina attempts to picture his face during one of her moments of fear, "the image appeared in her vision like a snap-shot. . . . He was a photograph in her mind, with the static pose which characterized him." In contrast to the erratic and impulsive gestures of his wife, "there was a rock-like centre to his movements, a sense of perfect gravitation. His emotions, his thoughts revolved around a fixed centre like a well organized planetary system" (*Spy*, 15 and 18).

The name of Nin's heroine—Sabina—is both appropriate and ironic; she is a seducer by temperament, a victim by conscience. The presentation of these conflicting aspects of her nature is also accomplished through the use of skillfully chosen images and symbols. Associated with the seductive qualities of the heroine are the images of fever and disguise. Sabina is usually dressed in "red and silver" or purple. Her eyes are painted with "kohl"—coal dust. One of her lovers calls her his "firebird"; another paints her as "*a mandrake with fleshly roots, bearing a solitary purple flower in a purple-bell-shaped corolla of narcotic flesh.*" When the lie detector looks at Sabina, his impression is that "*everything will burn.*"

By making Sabina an actress, Nin has found a convenient way of portraying the deceptive nature of her heroine. In addition to the deceit she thus practices with gestures, Sabina is also an expert in the application of cosmetics, and in the selection of costumes. "Multiple acts of composure and artifice" precede and follow each of the little dramas she enacts with her lovers.

The impression of Sabina as victim of her own conscience is created by the use of images associated with guilt and punishment. "She was compelled by a confessional fever which forced her into lifting a corner of the veil, and then frightened when anyone listened too attentively. She repeatedly took a giant sponge and erased all she had said by absolute denial, as if this confusion were in itself a mantle of protection" (*Spy,* 10). Betrayal, treason, crime, arrest, enemy, evil, and fear appear as often in Nin's novel as they would in a police report, but in *A Spy in the House of Love,* of course, each word carries more than the usual emotional charge, and each is symbolic.

One of her lovers "sought to capture the recurrences of certain words in her [Sabina's] talk, thinking that they might be used as keys" (*Spy,* 118-119). The searcher for the structural principles in Nin's novel is wise to follow his example: by closely observing the recurring images and words he will be in possession of one key to the organization of her novel.

Phrasal repetition, a technique associated with musical composition, is also used as a structural principle in this novel. In the opening movement of *A Spy in the House of Love,* Sabina as siren is introduced in the vivid passage beginning "Dressed in red and silver. . . ." In the closing movement of the novel the passage is repeated, and prefaced by the statement: "Sabina began to look . . . as she had looked the first time Jay had seen her" (*Spy,* 7 and 114). The description of Sabina as fugitive is treated similarly. In the opening movement, Sabina "could not sit still. She talked profusely and continuously. . . ." In the closing section the passage is introduced with the adverbial phrase, "After seven years," and is then repeated verbatim (*Spy,* 7 and 115). By *enclosing* her novel in this way, Nin is able to give her novel a "finished" look without destroying the impression of flow. Furthermore, since this device emphasizes and is derived from the mobility-stability theme (the episodes within the repeated passages present the idea of mobility, the repetition brings the idea of stability), once again "the form is created by the meaning"—Nin's foremost theory of structure.

In this work, as in all of Nin's novels, symbolism is given the three-fold function of condensing, defining, and unifying the heroine's experiences. For example, to eliminate the need for lengthy explanations of the meaning of Sabina's relationship with each of her paramours, Nin either invests each of the lovers with a particular symbolic quality or associates him with a simple but symbolically significant object.

Philip, the first of the lovers, is an opera singer who reminds Sabina of the famous Don Juan. By emphasizing the attraction Sabina feels for these mythical qualities, Nin is able, in a very short space, to concretely present Sabina in her Cinderella role. Mambo's name as well as his drum are used to give the reader a vivid impression of the "native" Sabina and the nature of the role she plays when it is this self that comes to the fore. John, the third of her lovers, is an aviator and a gunner. When Sabina sleeps with him she "sleeps with war." Donald, the anemic adolescent, is a collector of "empty cages." He tells Sabina he is determined to keep them empty until he finds "a unique bird" he once saw in his dream. When he suggests that Sabina is that bird, the heroine becomes aware that she is "moulting"—shedding her role as siren and assuming the role of mother.

But the most important contribution of symbolism to the form of *A Spy in the House of Love* is to be found in Nin's use of Duchamp's "Nude Descending a Staircase" as her central structural symbol. In the novel the picture is described as follows: "Eight or ten outlines of the same woman, like many multiple exposures of a woman's personality, neatly divided into many layers, walking down the stairs in unison" (*Spy,* 123). Structurally, each of the episodes in Nin's novel corresponds to one of the individual outlines. All the outlines taken together—the actual picture—correspond to the complete novel. Because this symbolic picture also has thematic implications—the outlines represent mobility, the total picture, stability—once again Nin reveals that in practice she is true to her theory that in the new novel "form is born of theme."

In addition to the individual form that each of the Nin novels inherently possesses, her work also has a canonical form. In the introductory comments to *Children of the Albatross* Nin writes: "The books can . . . be read separately or can be considered as parts of a tapestry."[31] The whole tapestry of the Nin canon depicts "woman at war with herself." The individual novels, therefore, may be considered as variations on this theme. In this context there are four basic variations corresponding to the basic problems of the modern woman. The Sabina stories ("Sabina," *A Spy in the House of Love*) are concerned with restlessness, the desire to become attached and yet to remain free, the need to change without losing one's identity. The problem explored in the Stella novelette is the frustration involved in trying to make the personal image conform to the social one. Lillian's role in the novels in which she appears ("This Hunger," *Seduction of the Minotaur*) is to dramatize not only the need for sexual satisfaction but the balance between the sexes that such a fulfillment demands. Djuna and her experiences (*Winter of Artifice,* "This Hunger," *Four-Chambered Heart*) reveal the triple need in woman for the child, the father, and the lover, and the necessity for keeping these roles unconfused. In this way, each of the individual novels presents one face of the heroine of the canon, Woman, who, to Nin, is never a single personality but "a distracting harem."

The chronological order of her work also suggests a developmental pattern which reinforces the theme and structure of the individual works. From her first creative work in 1936 to the most recently published novel, 1964, there is a steady progression from subjectivity to objectivity both on the part of the narrator in the novel and in Nin's own handling of her materials. That such a plan was more intentional than accidental is indi-

---

[31] Nin, "Introduction" to *Children of the Albatross,* p. [iii].

cated by her "Preface" to the first edition of *Under a Glass Bell*. After describing dream literature as an "opium" she writes, "The Spanish War awakened me. I passed out of romanticism, mysticism, and neuroticism into reality. . . . But it is necessary to understand, to be aware of what caused the suffering which made such an opium essential. . . ."[32] While this perhaps is a remark concerning Nin the woman, in the following excerpt from "The Writer and the Symbols" Nin the artist speaks similarly:

> This quest of the self through the intricate maze of modern confusion is the central theme of my work. But you cannot reach unity and integration without patiently experiencing first of all all the turns of the labyrinth of falsities and delusions in which man has lost himself. And you cannot transcend the personal by avoiding it, but by confronting it and coming to terms with it.[33]

Very much as Joyce, in *A Portrait of the Artist as a Young Man*, dramatizes the growth of the artist as a technical movement from first to third person narration, Nin begins her work with the lyrical prose-poem, *House of Incest*, written as first person narrative, and ends with *Collages*, an artist's notebook composed of objective portraits and which is the most satiric and objective of all her works.

In his attempt to provide an adequate definition of "form" in the novel, Percy Lubbock, in *The Craft of Fiction*, writes: "Though we readily talk of the book as a material work of art, our words seem to be crossed by a sense that it is rather a process, a passage of experience, than a thing of size and shape."[34] This feeling of "passage" rather than of precise shape is especially the impression that a Nin novel evokes. Instead of the "two and thirty chapters" of the traditional novel, she creates a "flowing inner chronicle"; instead of a series of novels, she produces *"a roman fleuve."*

---

[32] Quoted by Robert Gorham Davis in "The Fantastic World of Anaïs Nin," *New York Tribune Book Review* (March 28, 1948), p. 24. The idea for such a canonical form seems to have occurred to Nin in the early stages of her career, as the question of subjective *versus* objective writing is a constant concern in *The Diary: 1931-1934*.

[23] "The Writer and the Symbols," p. 37.

[34] Percy Lubbock, *The Craft of Fiction* (London, 1924), p. 15.

V

☆ ☆ ☆ ☆ ☆

Modern Psychomachia

In that classic of novel criticism, *Aspects of the Novel,* E. M. Forster defines character as "to whom it happened," describes characterization as the construction of "word-masses" and entitles the chapter dealing with this aspect of the novel, "People."[1] In the fiction of Anaïs Nin the definition and description are applicable, but the title, strictly speaking, is not, a consideration that many of her reviewers either fail to recognize or refuse to accept as valid when they do. Isaac Rosenfeld, in "Psychoanalysis as Literature," calls Nin a "thoroughgoing mechanist" and complains that her characters are without personality, "mere personifications of neurotic anxiety."[2] Diana Trilling makes the "cute" critical slip of calling Nin the psychoanalyst and her characters "patients" and then goes on to explain why she finds these characters lacking in the attributes usually associated with "people":

> For instance, we are told of Hejda that, having been born in the Orient, her face was veiled through her early years, but we are not told the name of the country of her birth; or, in connection with Lillian, Miss Nin suddenly mentions a husband and children, but because neither husband nor children influence Lillian's emotional development Miss Nin doesn't consider it pertinent to tell us anything about them.[3]

Both of these critics are looking for "round" characters such as are usually found in the traditional novel, and not finding them, they conclude that Anaïs Nin's creative powers are limited. Or on the other hand, noticing that she is dealing with exaggerated psychological states, they hastily attach the label "psychoanalysis" to her writing and assume that here is simply a fictionized application of Freud's discoveries. But there is a reason why Nin leaves out "so much that you are accustomed to find in character novels" and consequently why she is *not* a "thoroughgoing mechanist." Basically, it is a question of the difference between the literary and the mathematical concept of type and plot.

In naturalistic fiction the setting of the novel is essentially laboratorial; the novelist assumes the posture of the scientist, with his theme functioning as a hypothesis. Characters are chosen according to their statistical averageness, incidents are structured to prove the hypothesis, and the finished

---

[1] E. M. Forster, *Aspects of the Novel* (London, 1964), pp. 51-71.
[2] Isaac Rosenfeld, "Psychoanalysis as Literature," *New Republic* (December 17, 1945), p. 844.
[3] Diana Trilling, "Fiction in Review," *Nation* (January 26, 1946), p. 105.

product resembles a sociological study with a few literary embellishments.

Two things alone could prompt a reader to place Nin in such company: first, the knowledge that she had first-hand experience with psychoanalysis; and second, the failure to recognize the tradition in which her work belongs. Since both reflect critical myopia in general, suffice it to say here that Nin's experiences are only the raw materials that she fashions in accordance with artistic, not clinical, principles. There is a difference between a case-history and a literary study of frustration. Her characters and incidents are always "born of theme" and are never manipulated to support an external scientific law.

Because in the Nin metaphysic the dream is as important as, if not more important than physical encounters, and because the significance of an object is as important as its empirical form, her characters can not be expected to function like "real people." Their allegiance is not to society but to the "cities of the interior." It is this difference in point of view and emphasis rather than any lack of ability that accounts for the "strangeness" of her characters and that distinguishes them from the specimens of the naturalists.

In attempting to "clarify some misunderstandings that have occasionally blocked the response" to her work Nin writes: "There is a purpose and form behind my partial, impressionistic, truncated characters. The whole house, or the whole body, the entire environment, may not be there, but we know from modern painting that a column can signify more than a whole house, and that one eye can convey more than two at times."[4] The key words are "partial" and "signify," indicating on one hand the type of portraiture to be found in her novels, and on the other hand the type of role that her characters will play.

E. M. Forster in theory and Charles Dickens in practice have shown that characters need not be "round" to be interesting and convincing; and if Nin's characters must be defined according to accepted literary standards it is in the category of "flat" but "vibrating" that they belong. But to discuss her characters in these terms would do more to support Forster's theory than to explain Nin's art.

There is a much older race of *homo fictus* to which the lineage of her characters may be traced: the *dramatis personae* of the *Psychomachia* of Prudentius and its offshoot, the Christian morality plays. In these early literary forms personified abstractions of vice and virtue engaged in conflict for "Everyman's" soul. In the modern *psychomachia* of Nin personifications of the basic passions battle for supremacy in the female psyche.[5] It would be unwise to suggest that Nin consciously modelled her characters according to this ancient dramatic technique but it is obvious that she was

---

[4] *Realism and Reality*, p. 13.
[5] Cf. Maxwell Geismar, "Temperament vs. Conscience," *Nation* (July 24, 1954), pp. 75-76.

guided by a similar concept of the significance and consequently of the need to externalize the inner conflict. "Woman at war with herself" is the unifying theme of her work, and in the "Prologue" to *Ladders to Fire* she explains that in order to develop this theme "it is necessary to return to the origin of the confusion, which is woman's struggle to understand her own nature." Because the *psychomachic* struggle is a battle not between the hero and external forces but between "the various selves" it should now be obvious why Nin's characters have, on one level at least, so little to do with "husbands and children."

In her "study" of D. H. Lawrence she explains the exaggerated and obsessional qualities of his characters as "a poetic means to an end, an end which is understanding":

> Lawrence does not create what we generally understand by a "character," that is, a definitely outlined being who bears a resemblance to those we know. He does not give us such a clear outline because the personnages |sic] in his book are symbolical; he is more preoccupied with the states of consciousness and with subconscious acts, moods, and reactions. (*Lawrence*, 26)

As we have stated earlier, Nin's explanation is more applicable to her own practice than to Lawrence's. The "personnages" in her fiction are symbolical, and if they act according to a set pattern it is not because she is a mechanist but because they are, in the broad sense of the term, archetypal.

There are four main characters in the Nin novels, each portraying one aspect of the heroine—"woman"—who in this sense does not appear in the novels but is a composite of the four protagonists. Though again one would not like to make Nin appear more erudite than she really is, it is important to recognize that each of the main characters is described and acts according to one of the basic patterns associated with the theory of the four elements. Sabina, "dressed in red and silver . . . evoked the sounds and imagery of fire engines." Restlessness and feverishness are the passions she personifies; evasion and flight are her characteristic activities. In short, she is the modern choleric character. Stella, on the other hand, as her name indicates is cool and withdrawn, elusive and pale. Hers is a white world: "ivory satin bed, white nightgown, white rug—splendor, satin and space." She is the cool dreamer, a twentieth-century phlegmatic. Lillian, "always in a state of fermentation," always seeking for a mate to satisfy her sexual desires, represents the third "humour," the sanguine temperament. A "redhead," like Chaucer's Alisoun she requires more than the usual measure of sexual satisfaction. Djuna, like Stella, is also reticent but her reticence leads her to "muse" rather than withdraw. A Hamlet-like figure, she describes herself as "a pale watcher." Thus she represents the melancholic temperament. The effect of the theory of the four humours for Ben Jonson was to make his characters types and consequently his comedy "unrealistic" but his drama extremely effective and therefore psychologically true. Nin's practice involves a similar polar effect.

The second way in which Nin types her characters is equally traditional and poetic. "There is almost something mythic about the characters," observes Duane Schneider,[6] an observation he could have supported by simply considering their names. Sabina, for example, calls up the famous "rape of the Sabine women"; Stella means star, of course, and consequently evokes the legends of those luminary virgins, Diana and Artemis; Lillian's name may be traced to the "other" Eve, Lilith; and Djuna phonetically takes her place as the great mother of the gods, Juno. As with the elemental schematization, the central value of such a method is that it gives her work a timeless quality and makes it poetic rather than clinical.

Lastly, each of Nin's characters may also be viewed as symbolic of a specific complex or type of behavior. It is here that psychoanalysis comes into play, or rather Nin's attempt to modernize the old psychology. Sabina, a female Raskolnikov, is a schizophrenic with a conflicting will to crime and punishment. Lillian is an extrovert with an over-developed libido, while Djuna, her opposite, is basically an introvert and sexually frigid. Stella, with a "screen face" of wax but an unimpressionable body, vacillates between pleasure and pain in her role as masochist. The major contribution of this technique, like the first, is its depersonalizing effect; Stella is by name a female character, but as a phlegmatic or as a masochist she represents man as well as woman.

The problem for each of these characters is to reconcile her basic temperament with her other lesser passions or with a socially-formed conscience. The minor characters in the novels serve as catalysts to precipitate and localize the struggle. Since each of the novels is narrated from the limited point of view of the heroine, the conflict is usually revealed in the interaction of the "two voices." Frequently, however, the conflict is externalized and presented in dramatic terms. In *A Spy in the House of Love,* for example, Sabina "calls up" the "lie-detector," a character who then functions as her personified conscience. In *Winter of Artifice,* Part II, Djuna projects her other self into the figure of "the Voice": "this talking to a man she could not see was like a dialogue with a Djuna much greater than the everyday Djuna, a Djuna she felt at times as clearly as one feels the pushing of the wind on street corners" (*Winter,* 88). Lillian, in *Seduction of the Minotaur,* chooses Dr. Hernandez as her externally projected conscience: "The first friend she had made in Golconda, choosing him in preference to the engineer and the night-club manager, resembled, at least in his role, a personage she had known who was nicknamed "The Lie Detector" (*Seduction,* 8).

---

[6] Duane Schneider, "The Art of Anaïs Nin," *Southern Review,* VI, N.S. (Spring, 1970), p. 510.

The functional role of these symbolic characters is to bring the reader into direct contact with the kind of experience that would be only implicit in a standard "character novel." Like sacrificial victims, her characters are magnified so that their sensitivity may be proportionately increased, and thus the reader participating in their sufferings may be relieved in a cathartic manner of his own implicit neurosis. That such was Nin's intention may be seen from the following explanation in "The Writer and the Symbols": "If such writing at first appears esoteric it is only because it reflects a spiritual underground life of which most people are unaware, and it is unfortunate that they usually only become aware of its existence when, by excessive denial and repression, it grows distorted into neurosis and begins to fester like an abcess [sic] of the soul."[7] As the word "neurosis" suggests, the specific technique has a modern explanation, but as the words "soul" and "spiritual" indicate, Nin recognizes an older and more poetic rationale.

In addition to their psycho-moral characteristics Nin's characters also have external-practical attributes that make them ideally suited to the playing of symbolic roles. These they hold in common: all are women, all are artists, all are generally known only by their first names.

Anaïs Nin's choice of female protagonists is, on the one hand, a result of her awareness that her perception is basically intuitive and sensitive, and thus a perfect device for analyzing the "feminine mystique." On the other hand, since she sees woman as more elemental than man, and since it is the restrictions civilization imposes upon natural man and the consequences which concern her, the female figure is a poetically necessary vehicle.

In a similar way there is a thematic and aesthetic reason for her choice of artistic occupations for her heroines. Since she is not concerned with the social scene but with psychological states she requires characters who are excessive rather than average in their reactions and responses. "Do people really swing from one extreme emotion to another in so short a span?" she asks in her discussion of Lawrence's characters; "We know that poets do," she answers. "Lawrence is giving his characters an extreme sensibility, the power of poets" (*Lawrence,* 25). As usual, the explanation best describes her own practice. Her characters are artists not because she is attempting to write a *kunstlerroman* or because she is concerned only with the poetic personality but because she believes that the artist embodies the exaggerated feelings of the common man. And this does not mean that she is striving for realism, but rather that she recognizes the poetic significance of the stereotype. It is the archetypal concept of *the* artist, not the historical actuality that governs her practice.

A second reason for making her protagonists artists is that in Wag-

---

[7] "The Writer and the Symbols," p. 36.

nerian fashion Nin is searching for the comprehensive art form. Not only does she want a fusion of poetry and prose but also a literary synthesis of other media:

> The craft of writing can include all the others. A writer can possess the eye of a painter as Proust did, the ear of a musician as Joyce did, the rhythm of a dancer as Isabel Bolton's prose has in "Do I wake or sleep." He can possess the antennae of a clairvoyant, as Isaak Dinesen did in her book on Africa: the prophetic qualities of a fortune teller as Huxley did in "Brave New World." He can have the sense of form of a sculptor.
>
> The knowledge of textures of a dress designer, an eye for scenic arrangements of the stage director. He has to be an architect to house his characters, an etymologist, a botanist. He needs all the arts and sciences to reveal all the aspects of man.[8]

While the architectonics of the work must accomplish the greater part of this desired synthesis the use of an artistic protagonist provides direction and coherence, and prevents the technique from being decorative or the form mechanical.

Lastly, since the art form partakes of the outerworld in the sense that it is an externalized expression and of the dream or inner landscape in the sense that it is impulsive in origin, artists are to Nin exemplary of the fusion that is basic to her conception of reality.

The final characteristic that Nin's characters have in common is their lack of surnames. The reasons are many and obvious. First name acquaintance indicates on one hand, intimacy and subjectivity, on the other, lack of externality and "realistic" status. Also, since many of the names that Nin chooses for her characters are in themselves symbolic, last names would merely confuse the issue. It is psychological rather than "real" property that interests Nin.

In order to portray her symbolic characters, and through them her theory of reality as fusion of appearance and significance, Nin uses an old and effective technique of characterization. The following description of Lillian, from *Ladders to Fire,* is well equipped to reveal her method:

> Lillian was always in a state of fermentation. Her eyes rent the air and left phosphorescent streaks. Her large teeth were lustful. One thought of a negress who had found a secret potion to turn her skin white and her hair red.
>
> As soon as she came into a room she kicked off her shoes. Necklaces and buttons choked her and she loosened them, scarves strangled her and she slackened them. Her hand bag was always bursting full and spilled over. (*Ladders,* 67)

Joseph Frank describes such images as the kind that "analyze without dissociating . . . they describe character but at the same time hold fast to the

---

[8] *Ibid.,* p. 34.

unity of personality without splintering it to fragments in trying to seize the secret of its interpretation."[9] This, of course, is exactly what Nin is striving to achieve—and she succeeds admirably. "The Mouse was a small woman with thin legs, big breasts, and frightened eyes," she begins one of her short stories (*Bell,* 26), and the reader is immediately and simultaneously aware of the woman's physical appearance and psychological make-up.

Another method of characterization that she uses is that frequently associated with Henry James—characterization through environment. The reticent Djuna lives in a house in which there is a permanently "sealed room." "Even in the bathroom there were no medicine bottles on the shelves proclaiming: castor oil, cold cream. She had transferred all of them to alchemist bottles, and the homeliest drug assumed the air of a philtre" (*Children,* 39). Michael, the anemic homosexual, in *Seduction of the Minotaur,* lives in a ruined convent in a Mexican ghost-town.

A variant of this relief technique is Nin's use of cosmetics and clothes as an index to character. Lillian appears as a "tumult in orange red yellow and green quarelling with each other" (*Ladders,* 69). To Stella hats "demanded that a role be played to its maximum perfection. So each time she had reached into the joyous hat exhibit, looked at the treasured hats, she took again the little skull cap, the unobtrusive page and choir-boy cap" (*Ladders,* 19). The "spy" in the "House of Love," Sabina, applies her make-up, explaining while she performs the task both the method and reason for such a disguise:

> The eyebrow pencil was no mere charcoal emphasis on blond eyebrows, but a design necessary to balance a chaotic asymetry [sic]. Make up and powder were not simply applied to heighten a porcelain texture, to efface the uneven swellings caused by sleep, but to smooth out the sharp furroughs designed by nightmares, to reform the contours and blurred surfaces of the cheeks, to erase the contradictions and conflicts which strained the clarity of the face's lines, disturbing the purity of its forms. (*Spy,* 11)

Just as in the settings of her novels there are no structures that are not symbolic, so there are no physical descriptions applied to her characters that do not indicate a psychological equivalent.

One of Nin's critics observes that "the actual gestures and words of her characters are only a small and not too significant part of the meaning's whole."[10] Since the meaning lies in the struggle itself, and since the characters are symbolic rather than "realistic," Nin offers an alternative to the standard idea of the novel as portraiture. She suggests that her characters

[9] Joseph Frank, "Spatial Form in Modern Literature," *Sewanee Review,* LIII (1945), Part II, p. 437.

[10] "Cities of the Interior," in *Two Cities* (May 15, 1960), p. 103.

and their manner of acting resemble the sculptor Brancusi's "bird in space."[11] As the title implies, it is neither bird nor space that the artist is interested in but the interaction of the two—the impression of flight. Nin is striving for a similar unique effect; not a record of words nor a photograph, not the "illusion of life" but the impression of a struggle. Consequently, like the sculptor, she eliminates all unnecessary external characteristics and reshapes the "body." Refashioned in this manner her characters are equipped to make their voyages into "the cities of the interior."

For a closer look at character and characterization in Nin's fiction one might examine the appearance and experiences of an individual protagonist —Lillian—in the novels in which she appears—*Ladders to Fire* and *Seduction of the Minotaur.*

Like all of Nin's heroines, Lillian is an artist, and the type of art form with which she is associated is the essential key to her character. Lillian is a *musician*. Since a musician is an artist who must come into bodily contact with his medium in order to create, by choosing a musical career for her heroine Nin suggests that Lillian's dominating passion is one that must find outlet in physical rather than intellectual relationships. In *Ladders to Fire* one of Lillian's musical performances is described as a *"corps a corps"* [sic] (*Ladders*, 138).

The type of instrument that Lillian plays is also a characterizing device. The piano is a large instrument played by means of keys and hammers. By making her a pianist, therefore, Nin emphasizes the emotional and physical magnitude of her heroine: "The piano under her strong hands became small like a child's piano. She overwhelmed it, she tormented it, crushed it. She played with all her intensity, as if the piano must be possessed or possess her" (*Ladders*, 137-138).

Finally, the musical genre in which Lillian is proficient is also a key to her character. As a child, we are told, Lillian had been trained as a classical artist, but when she became a woman she turned to jazz. "Classical music could not contain her improvisations, her tempo, her vehemence." She selects jazz because "jazz [is] the music of the body." "In the world there was a conspiracy against improvisation. It was permitted only in jazz" (*Seduction*, 6 and 115). In summary, by making Lillian a jazz pianist Nin has established her heroine's role as the libidinous and sensual "Woman Agonistes."

Part of Lillian's problem is to recognize and accept her Eve-Lilith temperament in a healthy creative way. *Seduction of the Minotaur* is concerned primarily with this aspect of her struggle. But before the heroine is permitted such an anagnorisis she must endure a long period of suffering, self-doubt, and frustration. It is this period that is presented in *Ladders to Fire*, and which should be examined first.

---

[11] *Realism and Reality*, p. 14.

Lillian, though highly sensual and in need of strong sexual stimulation, is not aggressive by nature. "Deep down" she has the normal female desire to be conquered; "Deep down, what her nature wanted was to be made to yield" (*Ladders, 75*). But two things prevent Lillian from playing the normal female role: fear that the male will not allow her to achieve her proper female expression because of his inadequacies, and fear that she, the woman, is also inadequate, fear that her nature is not a satisfactory one. The two fears, both a result of lack of self-awareness, work together to turn Lillian the passionate female into Lillian the unhappy, aggressive, masculine warrior or the equally unhappy, dominating, protective guardian of others. In each of Lillian's heterosexual relationships it is this transformation and the reasons for it that are dramatized.

In terms of her development (the episode is related in a flash-back), Lillian's first lover is the anonymous youth she is to meet at a specific time on her bicycle. But fear that she may arrive before him—indicative of her fear of both her own and his inadequacies—increases Lillian's pedaling tempo, and consequently her fears are justified. She does arrive too soon. Lillian's reaction is to blame herself for playing Romeo instead of Juliet: "She had leaped, she had acted Romeo, and when woman leaped she leaped into a void" (*Ladders, 110*).

The pattern is repeated with slight variation in Lillian's second heterosexual relationship. To compensate for what she feels to be her basic failing, her overt and active sexuality, Lillian chooses as her second lover "a pale passive, romantic, anaemic figure, garbed in grey and timidity," Gerard. Of course this relationship aggravates rather than alleviates Lillian's distrust of both the male and herself. Again she has leaped into a void; she is forced "to play the lover alone, giving the questions and the answers too." Unable to see that it is the nature of the relationship itself that is at fault, Lillian blames herself: "I did not arouse his love. . . . And she began to make a long list of self-accusations." Furthermore, because this time "she had been the aggressor so she was the more seriously wounded." Lillian now becomes belligerent and defensive in addition to being aggressive. "She was living on a plane of war" (*Ladders, 69 and 74*).

Lillian's relationship to her husband is also characterized by imbalance. Lillian plays the role of matriarch; her husband, she feels, is just another child. But not only is the marital relationship imbalanced; it is also incomplete. Like Sabina, Lillian feels that her husband has not accepted her as the woman she has become, but rather he is in love only with the woman she was when he first married her. To dramatize Lillian's feelings concerning this stasis, Nin introduces the Poe-esque episode of the man next door: the man has been discovered cohabitating with the dead body of his wife. Unable to stand the "odor of death, the image of death," in her own home, Lillian leaves her husband and family.

Jay, the next and last of her lovers in this novel, is as fickle as her husband was constant, as active sexually as Gerard was passive. But his relationship to Lillian is based strictly on appetite, not the appetite of a man but the appetite of a child. Instead of being desired as a lover, Lillian is wanted as a mother: "His taking of her was not to take or master her. He was the lover inside of the woman, as the child is inside of the woman" (*Ladders,* 121). Whereas her husband's sexual performance had been inadequate because he always remained "outside of her," because he had only been able to "visit" not to fuse, Jay is an unsatisfactory lover because he wants to "lodge" inside her. He gives Lillian "the feeling of physical intermingling as she had had with her child."

Each of these heterosexual relationships leaves Lillian increasingly more dissatisfied and disillusioned. But at this point, although she knows there is a "deeper truth . . . she did not know what it was." The deeper truth, of course, is that Lillian has disguised her real self, has dressed herself in male clothes. It is this disguise that she is trying to mate, and thus every relationship is doomed from the start. But Lillian as yet does not know this; she only knows she is unhappy. And in this mood she turns to homosexual relationships.

Lillian's associations with the members of her own sex, however, are not designed to reveal lesbian qualities either in herself or in the others. On the contrary, from each of her female friends Lillian attempts to extract the particular female quality that has enabled the other woman to enjoy a satisfactory relationship with a male. This, Djuna, frequently the spokesman for Nin, explains: "She wants something of me that only a man can give her. But first of all she wants to become me, so that she can communicate with man. She is doing it through me" (*Ladders,* 107). From Djuna, "the essence of femininity," Lillian attempts to learn the "pleasure of capitulation," pleasures Lillian forfeited when she became the warrior, for "in war, conquest was imperative." "Sabina," the other woman to whom Lillian turns, "has no roots." "And I am strangling in my roots," says Lillian, as she compares herself and the other woman. What Lillian wants to learn of Sabina is freedom and mobility, the ability to delight in erotic adventures without needing to be constantly reassured of the eternal and affectionate aspects of the relationship.

The function of both of these women, thus, is to prepare Lillian for the awakening and rediscovery of her "dormant" and disguised female self. But in *Ladders to Fire* the heroine is not yet able to profit from her identification with them. She is still too possessed by the "demon doubt" and the monster, fear. Consequently, the novel closes with Lillian's "invisible hara-kiri":

A complete house-wrecking service. Every word, smile, act, silver jewel, lying on the floor, with the emerald green dress, and even Djuna's image ot Lillian to which she had often turned for comfort, that too lay shattered on the ground. Nothing to salvage. A mere pile of flaws. A little pile of ashes from a bonfire of self-criticism. (*Ladders,* 209)

Seduction of the Minotaur, as the symbolic title suggests, presents the final phase in Lillian's war with herself. The novel has a two-part structure: in the first or "Solar Barque" section, Lillian's old problems are reintroduced in her relationships to the other inhabitants of Golconda, and the knowledge needed to solve them is supplied through her conversations with Doctor Hernandez; in the concluding section of the novel, Lillian puts the two of them together—she objectively examines her problems and interprets and solves them in the light of her new found knowledge. Section one of the novel is thus the text; section two, the explication of it.

Lillian has come to Golconda to give "her ship, once and for all, its proper sea bed," that is, to rediscover her basic self so that she may live according to its demands, instead of in accordance with the laws of fear, as she has been doing. However, she mistakenly thinks she can accomplish this by forgetting the past; she wants to live like the natives who see "only the present." She wants to live conscienceless, entirely according to impulse.

But the road to self-awareness lies in the reconciliation of conscience and impulse; it demands the recognition and transcendence of the past, not an escape from it. To dramatize this aspect of Lillian's struggle is the purpose of her relationship with Doctor Hernandez. He plays the role of conscience to Lillian's role of fugitive.

Lillian resents the Doctor's probing of her motives for coming to Golconda. She tries to avoid him as much as possible in the opening episodes. But he does not disappear from the scene until he has thoroughly explained the doctrine of karma, the theory that the role one plays in the present is a reenactment of some unresolved conflict in the past. "You are a fugitive from truth," he tells Lillian; in Golconda "only the backdrop has changed" (*Seduction,* 29).

In the four episodes that follow this conversation Lillian is made to realize that his analysis of her situation is correct. In her attempt to free the American prisoner she reenacts the role she played with her husband, the role of manipulator and "courageous" liberator. Her relationship to the anemic Michael corresponds to her relationship with the passive Gerard. She realizes that she has chosen these half-men because of her fear that she could not satisfy a complete man. In her mothering of the child, Lietta, and the young student, Fred, she relives both her relationships to her own children and her relationship to the man-child Jay, and comes to realize that the dissatisfaction she has felt has been a result of her confusion of the maternal and sexual instincts.

Aware of and accepting the implications of these episodes, Lillian is ready "to return home." She returns to the village to "pack her unearthed treasures." But before she leaves, she feels she must do two things: first, she will "drink her last cup of flowing gold; second, she will seek out the Doctor," she will talk to him as "he wanted her to talk" (*Seduction*, 90-95). Lillian's first desire is symbolic of her recognition and appreciation of her body and sexual appetites, since "gold" and "Golconda" are synonymous with native and impulse in this context. The drink is referred to as "her last" to indicate that Lillian realizes now that as a civilized white woman it is impossible for her to live solely by instinct. Lillian's desire to seek out the Doctor is symbolic, on the other hand, of her willingness to accept her conscience and the consequent obligations.

It is on the evening of the first day in the New Year that Lillian walks up the hill to meet the Doctor. As she walks, she feels "more aware of her body," aware that it has become "a firm, elastic, balanced body, free in its movements." The Doctor is not there when she arrives, having been detained by "the natives' own religion of timelessness. They absolutely refused to live in obedience to clocks, and it was always their mood that dictated their movements." Lillian has also come to recognize that "clocks"—symbolic of all systems of measurement, scientific as well as social—can be limiting and enslaving.

As Lillian waits for the Doctor, suddenly the lights go out for a second. Shortly after, she learns that the Doctor is dead. Because Lillian has learned to fuse conscience and impulse, because she is now a whole woman, she no longer needs an external code or judge. "The last cup of gold" and the Doctor's death symbolize Lillian's new ability to fuse both extremes—conscience and impulse.

The last section of this novel is concerned with Lillian's journey homeward, that is, with the application of her new knowledge to her personal relationships. She now realizes that fear, resulting in her role as half-female-monster-half-male, was her minotaur. She realizes that having assumed the male role she gave birth to the "myth of her courage." And it was her own and others' "belief in this myth" that had prevented her from forming any satisfactory relationships. On the positive side, "The time was past when her body could be ravished from her by visitations from the world of guilt" (*Seduction*, 107). She is "reminded of the talmudic words: 'We do not see things as they are, we see them as we are'" (*Seduction*, 124). And now that she is whole, she can also see things clearly.

In *Ladders to Fire* Lillian is presented primarily as completely and subjectively involved in each of the novel's episodes; her statements are always questions. In the "Solar Barque" section of *Seduction of the Minotaur* she is still a participant but she is also capable of being the spectator in the dramas in which she is involved, and of extracting implications that pertain to her. Her characteristic statement in this section takes the form of an analytic summary. In the last section of *Seduction of the Minotaur*, Lillian is entirely a commentator; she juxtaposes her former problems and her new knowledge, and draws conclusions. Thus, in the novels in which she is protagonist, Lillian goes from participant to spectator to commentator—Nin's very effective way of revealing the three stages in her heroine's *psychomachia*.

VI

☆ ☆ ☆ ☆ ☆

Bread and the Wafer

In *Seduction of the Minotaur* the heroine smiles sarcastically and through her Anaïs Nin points accusingly at the "poor white man, wandering and lost in his proud possession of a dimension in which bodies became invisible to the naked eye." Unlike the native who sees with an immediate and physical vision, "the white man had invented glasses which made objects too near or too far, cameras, telescopes, spyglasses, objects which put glass between living and vision. It was the image he sought to possess, not the texture, the living warmth, the human closeness" (*Seduction,* 7). According to Nin, there are two kinds of writers who are more concerned with the image than the texture, with the word than with the flesh: the realist and the idealist.

The realist is the white man who looks through glasses that make objects too near—the camera and the spyglass (the modern equivalents of the mirror). Mechanical devices, they allow him to observe without becoming involved and to transfix living being into a two-dimensional image. In one of her short stories Nin mockingly describes one such literary photographer in action: "He entered her labyrinth with a notebook! If he annotated enough facts he would finally possess the truth." Later in the same story she pointedly comments on the limitations of such an approach: "Jay suspected that much was being hidden from him; it was not hidden by Sabina, but by his own purely external vision" ("Sabina," 51-52).

But it is not only because he is "a compiler of statistics, a census taker" that Nin objects to the realist; it is his medium of expression as much as his method of research that she objects to, that is, precise denotative prose. "People have lost their palate. All they can say is 'More'," complains the French *escoffier* Henri in one of the episodes in *Collages.* "They haven't lost their palate," answers Renate, "they have lost their tongue. They haven't lost their power to appreciate your cooking; what they have lost is the power of words. . . . We live in an Era of Basic English" (*Collages,* 57).

To Nin in the twentieth century as to Alexander Pope in the eighteenth century language is more than just an indication of civilization; it is an index to the moral and psychological condition of the age. The symptom and cause of decadence according to the poet of the *Dunciad* was the literary hack; the realist with his computer-like diction is both responsible for and indicative of our "impoverishment of language" according to the American artist. "Our western life has become mechanical, functional and devoid of meaning," she writes in "The Writer and the Symbols," and man "is in danger of becoming inarticulate" if he continues to live in "the deserts of bare and barren writing."[1] The only way to prevent this headlong plunge towards Houyhnhnmland is to reinvest language with the poetic and the sensuous.

That Nin's criticism of the present and her plan for the future are serious and practical and not merely the petty complaint of an antiquated aesthete is borne out by a timely editorial in *The Saturday Review*. In "The Computer and the Poet," the writer posits as "the essential problem of man in a computerized age . . . not solely how to be more productive, more comfortable, more content, but how to be more sensitive, more sensible, more proportionate, more alive." He concludes that it is the task of the artist to "help to keep man from making himself over in the image of his electronic marvels. For the danger is not so much that man will be controlled by the computer as that he may imitate it."[2] To Nin, as we have seen, one of the most obvious examples of this modern mimesis is the writing of the realists. "Reportage," she calls it in *Realism and Reality*, "facts stated objectively, scientifically, statistically without the artist's power to communicate their meaning."[3]

But of equal concern to Anaïs Nin is the idealistic tendency of modern man, the tendency to reduce life to a formula or mathematical equation. The idealist is the white man who sees through glasses that make objects too far, the cultural X-ray technician. Unlike the realist's preoccupation with material fact the idealist is obsessed with abstract fact, an extreme which is equally sterile and debilitating. Thus, although she admires the novelists André Gide and Aldous Huxley for their questioning of bourgeois attitudes, she dislikes their loyalty "only to the cool indifferent flux of intellectual curiosity." Against their scientific approach and intellectual style she juxtaposes the poetic techniques of Lawrence and finds the latter unquestionably superior: "Lawrence went at the reversal of values not with indifference but with religious fervor, and he *hit lower* than either Huxley or Gide. He hit the centre, the vulnerable centre of our bodies with his physical language, his physical vision. He hit us vitally" (*Lawrence, 33*).

When Nin dislikes an artist or a technique she usually finds some way of incorporating this prejudice into her creative writing. The following passage from *Ladders to Fire* may be taken as her tongue-in-cheek description of the modern Laputian and his artifact: "He passed on with royal detachment and gazed seriously for relief at the steel and wood mobiles turning gently in the breeze of the future, like small structures of nerves vibrating in the air without their covering of flesh, the new cages of our

---

[1] "The Writer and the Symbols," p. 35.

[2] "The Computer and the Poet," *Saturday Review* (July 23, 1966), p. 42. See also Storm Jameson, "The Writer in Contemporary Society," *The American Scholar* (Winter, 1965-66), pp. 67-77.

[3] *Realism and Reality*, p. 20.

future sorrows, so abstract they could not even contain a sob" (*Ladders,* 203).

To combat the "intellectual dressing of abstractions" on the one hand and "the impoverishment of language" on the other, then, is one of the reasons why Nin's writing is so highly sensuous and imagistic. But there is also a positive reason for her choice of such a medium. Echoing Emerson she writes: "At night every man dreams in the imagery of the poets."[4] Since to her the dream is as much a part of reality as the empirical real, and since poetry is the language that communicates directly to this unconscious aspect of reality, the medium of the artist who would "see life whole" requires "a fusion of two extremes which have been handled separately, on one side by the poets, and on the other side by the so-called realists."[5] The three major poetic devices that she uses to accomplish this fusion are rhythm, imagery and diction.

While stream-of-consciousness is one of the basic effects for which she strives, she constantly experiments with prose rhythms to vary the pace and to add a dramatic tone. Frequently she accomplishes this by introducing a short *staccotoed* phrase or sentence between the slow and regular rhythm of two long paragraphs. Or she may rely on the difference of inflection in a question and an answer, or the question may function as the emotional climax and the rhythmical pause: "She is waiting for him. She has waited for him for twenty years. He is coming today. She has almost grown old with waiting. Will he be old?" (*Winter,* 1). The repetition of "She is-She has, He is-She has" is like a carefully balanced see-saw which is suddenly arrested in the clipped and monosyllabic question. Similarly, one might notice the way the metrical patterns of the first and third sentences are lengthened into those of the second and fourth, thereby conveying not only the sense but the sensation of the passing of time. Like the prose of Henry James, Nin's writing can be fully appreciated only by a sensitive reader; but whereas James requires attention to grammatical convolutions, Nin depends upon rhythmical variations. Richard McLaughlin observes that "in revealing to us the rhythms of the poet she displays a cascade of sounds which all but crowd out of our heads the demand that her words should at all times have meaning."[6] This is especially evident in her early work, *House of Incest;* and it is an extreme that must count as a fault:

> Come away with me, Alraune, come to my island. Come to my island of red peppers sizzling over slow braseros, Moorish earthen jars catching the gold water, palm trees, wild cats, fighting, at dawn a donkey sobbing, feet on coral reefs and sea-anemones, Melisande's hair hanging over the balcony at the Opera Comique, inexorable diamond sunlight, heavy nerveless hours. . . . (*House,* 19)

---

[4] *Ibid.,* p. 15.
[5] *On Writing,* p. 23.
[6] Richard McLaughlin, "Shadow Dance," *Saturday Review* (December 20, 1947), p. 16.

But when she exercises a little more craft and is not carried away by emotional exuberance, even in the same work, she is able to create a complex of rhythm and imagery that is both emotionally and intellectually satisfying: "Trees reclining, woods shining, and the forest trembling with rebellion so bitter I heard its wailing within its deep forest consciousness. Wailing the loss of its leaves and the failure of transmutation" (*House*, 42). Here the rhythm supports rather than assaults the sense.

Frequently rhythm is used to reinforce the description of a character, as in the following passage from "Stella": "An air of the unformed waiting to be formed, an air of evasion waiting to be catalyzed. Indefinite contours, a wavering voice capable of all tonalities, tapering to a whisper, an air of flight waiting to be captured" (*Ladders*, 18). And to see how very skillful is Nin's use of this technique one should contrast this passage with the rhythmical pattern used in the description of Stella's opposite in temperament, Sabina: "Dressed in red and silver, she evoked the sounds and imagery of fire engines as they tore through the streets of New York, alarming the heart with the violent gong of catastrophe; all dressed in red and silver, the tearing red and silver cutting a pathway through the flesh. The first time he looked at her he felt: *everything will burn!*" (*Spy*, 7). Both heroines are elusive and evasive, but Sabina is a heady siren whereas Stella is a fairy-like maiden. Thus, while the rhythmical pattern used in the description of both is sweeping and flowing, in the Stella passage it resembles a gentle river, in the Sabina passage, a gushing torrent.

Since the most basic rhythms in life are those of the pulse and copulation, Nin experiments with ways of making the sexual encounters of her heroines rhythmically perceptible. To prepare the reader for Sabina's "complicity" the narrator begins with the pathetic fallacy rendered in a slow heavy chant:

> Beneath the delicate skin, the tendrils of secret hair, the identations [sic] and valleys of flesh, the volcanic lava flowed, desire incandescent, and where it burned the voices of the blues being sung became a harsh wilderness cry, bird and animal's cry of pleasure and cry of danger and cry of fear and cry of childbirth and cry of wound pain from the same hoarse delta of nature's pits.

Then the tempo increases:

> They fled from the eyes of the world, the singer's prophetic, harsh, ovarian prologues. Down the rusty bars of ladders to the undergrounds of the night propitious to the first man and woman at the beginning of the world, where there were no words by which to possess each other, no music for serenades, no presents to court with, no adornments, necklaces, crowns to subdue.

and comes to a climax with "but only one ritual, a joyous, joyous, joyous, joyous impaling of woman on man's sensual mast" (*Spy*, 36).[7] When she

---

[7] See also the description of Lillian's encounter with Jay (*Ladders*, p. 149), and Djuna's meeting with Paul (*Children*, pp. 91-92).

does not present the rhythm as directly as in the examples above, Nin uses an image of a rhythmical act to provide the proper tempo. Thus Lillian's first unsuccessful sexual experience is presented in terms of a bicycle trip. She and her lover are to leave their respective homes at the same time, and since they live equidistant from the prearranged meeting place, ideally they should but significantly do not arrive together. "Lillian started off. At first at a normal pace. She knew the rhythm of the boy. A rather easy, relaxed rhythm." But then her insecurities give rise to fear, "speeded her bicycle with the incredible speed of anxiety, a speed beyond the human body, beyond endurance. She arrived before him" (*Ladders,* 109-111).

Nin observes that modern writers have "forgotten how masterfully the ancients used charms to encourage salvation."[8] The use of a rhythmic style is one way that Nin attempts to revive the old literary religion. Another way is through the use of highly sensuous diction, language that makes "a physical impression." Rango plays his guitar,

> played it with the warm copper color of his skin, with the charcoal pupil of his eyes, with the underbrush thickness of his eyebrows, pouring into the honey-colored box the flavors of the open road on which he lived his gypsy life; thyme, rosemary, oregano, marjoram, and sage. Pouring into the resonant box the sensual swing of his hammock hung across the gypsy cart and the dreams born on his mattress of black horsehair. (*Heart,* [1-2])

The sterility and feverishness of the landscape and of the inhabitants of the *House of Incest* is evoked through a combination of onomatopoeic and imagistic words that allows the reader to perceive the emotional connotations of the scene long before the meaning is intellectually perceptible:

> Then she rushed out into the garden of dead trees, over the lava paths, over the micha schist, and all the minerals on her path burned, the muscovite like a bride, the pyrite, the hydrous silica, the cinnabar, the azurite like a fragment of benefic Jupiter, the malachite, all crushed together, pressed together, melted jewels, melted planets, alchemized by air and sun and time and space, mixed into mineral fixity, the fixity of the fear of death and the fear of life. (*House,* 43-44)

To Anaïs Nin, the medium of the artist is "not ink and paper but his body."[9] Through her emphasis on the sensual she makes her reader also use this medium. Sabina is painted as *"a mandrake with fleshly roots, bearing a solitary purple flower in a purple-bell-shaped corolla of narcotic flesh"* (*Spy,* 120). Isolina has "fur eyelashes" and "dilated eyes" (*House,* 33). As one critic replied to Nin's fear that modern writers are becoming "atrophied": "Miss Nin does not have to worry. . . . She is in more danger

---

[8] *On Writing,* pp. 25-26.
[9] *Realism and Reality,* p. 20.

of liquifying or bursting into flame than she is of turning into stone."[10]

"Listen to the language of the future," says a character in *A Spy in the House of Love* as he squeezes an automobile horn. "The word will disappear altogether and that is how human beings will talk to each other" (*Spy*, 114). To offset the realist's predilection for "basic English" Nin introduces the exotic, the rich, and the symbolic word wherever she can, gives her reader "a wafer in place of bread." Mazes become "labyrinths," temperaments are "simoun" or "sirocco," characters make "parabolic appearances," a born manipulator becomes "the Chess Player."

Retaining her native (French) grammatical constructions, she frequently uses compound nouns to lend a mythical atmosphere in her writing. Lillian makes her overtures to Djuna during "the night of gifts." Isolina is found in "the room of paintings." Lillian remembers her childhood home as "the house of no-smile."

Another reason for her preference for the unconventional word or phrase is her desire to prevent the reader from attempting to extract the "story" without benefiting from the sensuous effects. "The use of worn words to which there is no genuine reaction is like a senseless, unfelt, mechanical recitation of a rosary," she writes in her explanation of Lawrence's eccentricities (*Lawrence*, 65). And one way that she herself ensures that the reader is paying close attention is to interchange verbs and nouns and adjectives. "The boat undulated the aquatic plants," she writes in *Seduction of the Minotaur*. In *Ladders to Fire* Jay is described as "the proud chef playing gay scales of flavors, festooning the bread and wine with the high tastes of banquets." Later in the same novel, "On the round stairway they collided with Stella susurrating in a tafetta skirt."

The reason that Nin is able to maintain the reader's interest and understanding despite the frequent tenuousness of her themes is that her imagery is, with few exceptions, original, accurate and concrete. Concreteness is, of course, her way of being "realistic" and poetic in the same breath. "Greyness is no ordinary greyness," she writes in an attempt to depict weariness, "but a vast lead roof which covers the world like the lid of a soup pan" (*House*, 24). Since the bulk of her writing is concerned with feelings rather than with actions, the concrete image allows her to achieve the maximum economy and intensity, saves her from becoming abstract or verbose. Thus in one short sentence she is able to summarize Djuna's frustration at being stereotyped as an "angelic being" and her desire to reestablish her contact with the "real": "I want my dress torn and stained" (*Ladders*, 212). In a similar way she is able to present palpably and directly Lilith's early eroticism by allowing her to describe her feeling as a desire "to pass a violin bow between her legs" (*Winter*, 95).

---

[10] Harrison Smith, "Ladies in Turmoil," *Saturday Review* (November 30, 1946), p. 13.

Anaïs Nin's imagery is always accurate, but at times this accuracy is emotional rather than empirical. For example, although "gat-toothed" is now recognized as a pseudo-scientific indication of wantonness, large teeth have no necessary libidinal implications. Yet, in *Ladders to Fire,* when Nin writes of Lillian that her "large teeth were lustful," the reader is emotionally convinced of the accuracy of the description. The technique is similarly used in the following description of a happy old man: "The wrinkles of his face all ran upward, controlled by an almost perpetual smile." Like a cartoon, the image exaggerates the one upturned curve, disregarding the fact that perpetual smiling is more likely to create down-turned wrinkles. Despite the inaccuracy of the description, however, the reader receives the right impression.

Emotional rather than intellectual accuracy also characterizes her use of history, science, and tradition. In *Seduction of the Minotaur* the reader is told that Golconda had once been a pearl-fishing village, that "a ship-wrecked Spanish galley had scattered on the beach baptism dresses which the women of Southern Mexico had adopted as headgear" (*Seduction,* 8). Whether there is historical evidence for such an incident is beside the point; the difference in temperament and attitude between the civilized Spaniards and the primitive Mexicans is evoked by the image, and for Nin's purposes and the reader's understanding this is all that is required. Similarly in *Four-Chambered Heart,* one would not like to examine the following historic allusion too closely: "The Seine River began to swell from the rains, and to rise high above the watermark painted on the stones in the Middle Ages" (*Heart,* [24]). But it is the emotional implication, not the factual accuracy of the image, that she is interested in.

Usually Nin plunders eclectically and introduces her stolen treasure casually. A sentence from the *Talmud* is inserted with the same semblance of simplicity as when she drops the name of a modern jazz artist. An image from the Bible follows a comparison of tree roots to "the toes of Gulliver." Usually the technique is successful; the allusion enters unobtrusively, transfers its emotional charge, and fades back into the fabric of the narrative. But there are times when the reference seems to clutter rather than clarify, when it draws attention to the artist rather than to the meaning of the context. This is especially true of the astrological passages at the close of *Seduction of the Minotaur* and of the explanation of a bird's anatomy in *Children of the Albatross.*[11] These sections are as annoying and boring as

---

[11] See *Seduction,* pp. 130-136 and *Children,* pp. 61-62. Oliver Evans does not share my opinion that these passages clutter and distract. He feels that "the matter-of-factness of the scientific observations" provides an effective contrast to "the deeply personal quality of the reflections which they suggest and with which they alternate" ("Anaïs Nin," p. 223). Certainly Evans has correctly analyzed the theory behind Nin's practice, but in the passages cited above she fails to execute, as James would say. Like Henry Miller and, at times, Edmund Wilson, Evans is so appreciative of the artistry of Nin and so aware of her lack of recognition that he tends to exaggerate her merits rather than to critically emphasize them. But Nin is too good an artist to need biased criticism; she needs to be made known, not sold.

Dreiser's city-mapping, and indicate a violation of her own critical principle "to poetize and analyze simultaneously."

"Her feelings never deceived her," Nin writes of one of her characters, "It was only her imagination which deceived her. Her imagination could give a color, a smell, a beauty to things, even a warmth which her body knew very well to be unreal. . . . But her emotions were sincere and they revolted, they prevented her from getting lost down the deep corridors of her inventions."[12] Similarly, when Anaïs Nin gets lost in the corridors of her inventions it is always because she has inadvertently divorced feeling from imagination, the analysis from the poetic presentation. Hers is an essentially intuitive perception and when she allows it to be the controlling factor she never fails. Then, as one of her critics writes, "she is unequalled by anyone in this range since D. H. Lawrence and we know we are in the presence of literary genius."[13]

[12] Quoted by Vernon Young, from an early version of *Bell*, p. 429.
[13] Vernon Young, p. 428.

VII

☆ ☆ ☆ ☆ ☆

Backward and Forward

In an early chapter of her latest critical work, significantly titled *The Novel of the Future,* Anaïs Nin wisely observes: "At twenty we all created our own manifestoes. We were eager to be innovators. But the more culture we have, the more we know everything has roots in the past, and we owe something to our ancestors. The psychedelic world denies its debt to surrealism, but it is there nevertheless."[1] On the one hand, the "we" may be directed toward the youth of today and the statement then interpreted as Nin's tolerant admonition to them not to see themselves as independent but to admit the relevance of what she said and has to say. On the other hand, it may not be the "mod" audience but the young Nin towards whom the comment is directed. When Anaïs Nin began her literary career she was in her twenties, and saw her work as that of a young rebel. *The Novel of the Future,* written after a career of thirty-six years, may be viewed as the mature revaluation of her techniques and theories. Either way the passage points to the importance of the work in a study of Nin's writing: directly, it provides materials to answer the question of whether or not she has changed and why; indirectly, it enables one to check the interpretation of her theories and fiction presented throughout this study with her own.

Since *The Novel of the Future* must be generally classified as a critical work, one of the first topics to consider might be Nin's concept of criticism, and in this respect we have two materials for comparison: first, her initial study of D. H. Lawrence, and second, her other critical writings—*Realism and Reality, On Writing,* and "The Writer and the Symbols." The Lawrence book we have described as criticism of an essentially creative variety; its thesis took the form of a theme and its organization involved the literary stream-of-consciousness technique and the mythic genesis pattern. In *The Novel of the Future,* as far as presentation is concerned, the distinctly poetic element is absent. Structurally, the work employs a more logical developmental principle: she moves from her early writings to her latest publications and from specific focus upon her own work to analysis of that of other writers. Stylistically, she is as eclectic and spontaneous as she always has been, but now she writes in the interests of proving a point rather than in creating an effect. While it is not complete as an explanation, one might relate this type of change in criticism to the difference between the

---

[1] Nin, *Novel,* p. 36. (Since this chapter is concerned exclusively with this work, the abbreviated title will be omitted from the reference and identification will consist simply of the page number in parenthesis.)

early and late fiction, which as we have seen involved a careful movement from the subjective to the objective. "Proceed from the Dream Outward" is the title of the first chapter of *The Novel of the Future,* and both explicitly and implicitly it is the refrain of the entire work.

As far as the concept of criticism itself there is no essential difference between the early and the late Nin, although there is a difference in tone and emphasis. And herein, I think, we best find an explanation. In both *D. H. Lawrence: An Unprofessional Study* and *The Novel of the Future* she argues for a subjective response as the basis for true criticism, provided, that is, that the response is honest and that it leads away from itself to the impersonal and thus ultimately becomes real objectivity; in both works, conversely, she objects to the usual critic not because he is objective but because actually he is not, because he fails to acknowledge or to utilize his subjectivity. But in the Lawrence study it is the former argument that is positively upheld; in it her chief concern was to justify her "unprofessionalism," to champion subjectivity. In *The Novel of the Future* she is equally anti-academic, but now her emphasis is upon the subjectivity of most attempts to be objective, now her argument is negative and defensive: "I do feel we have very few objective critics. Many of them are motivated by their adhesion to political groups, others are academic and only apply the standards they learned in the past, still others are moralists" (103-104). In the early work, the fallacy of the objective was a positive premise, now it is made a negative proposition. "The concept of the infallible critic is childish. A critic has bad moods, subjective problems, neuroses, and a need to rationalize his personal likes and dislikes" (106). Before she argued that the unprofessional was more honest and hence accurate than the trained critic; now her argument is that the professionals are not professional enough: "The critic should be the intermediary, the interpreter. His personal likes and dislikes are of no value to anyone" (105). Since by "personal" she means petty and by "objective" she means unprejudiced, she is not contradicting her earlier defense of the subjective; it is not her thesis that has changed but, first, its presentation, and second, its direction. *D. H. Lawrence: An Unprofessional Study* is a poetic demonstration of the greater value of subjective criticism; *The Novel of the Future* is a prose exposé of so-called objective criticism and a defensive justification of subjective writing. The difference between the two works, then, can be explained in terms of the unsympathetic critical response Nin's work occasioned and the difference in material between the two studies. In the Lawrence book Nin's tactic was to use his art as a medium for her own ideas; in the later work her method is to use her own work and that of others like her in order to defend the theory of the "novel of the future," which, of course, is her own theory and practice.

To those who disliked her practice in the first place, consequently, *The Novel of the Future* will merely be a compounding of her errors, in particular providing further evidence of her critical irresponsibility. To them one might point out that just as in the Lawrence book Nin deliberately styled herself an "unprofessional," so in this work she makes no claims to detachment or to comprehensiveness but quite specifically indicates at the outset the purpose and scope of her study:

> The purpose of this book is to study the development and techniques of the poetic novel. I will try to evaluate some of the writers who have integrated poetry and prose. It is not a general study of writers, nor even of the writers I mention. It is a grouping, a relating of such writers to trends now acceptable and recognized under other names, "expanded consciousness," or if you prefer, "psychedelic" with emphasis upon *psyche*. (4)

The statement should also make pause those who consider the work simply as a repetition of her—by now—old fashioned theories. For as it implies, *The Novel of the Future* is as much a revaluation and an attempt to accommodate her theories to a new age as it is a summing up. The anecdote she introduces in the penultimate chapter applies as much to her situation as it does to that of Varèse: "Labels often alienate a writer from his readers. When Edgar Varèse was given a dinner to celebrate his seventy-fifth birthday, he was introduced as an avant-garde composer. He said: 'There is no avant-garde. The artist is always of his time but some people are a little late!'" (190). To Nin, the "people" are both the critics who condemned her innovations and the writers who think they are avant-garde—including in a peculiar way as we shall see, Nin the young critic.

In 1946, Anaïs Nin published her first critical manifesto, the pamphlet entitled *Realism and Reality*. The central issue of *The Novel of the Future* is also the difference between realism and reality, and parts of this early credo and its succeeding expressions—*On Writing* and "The Writer and the Symbols"—are taken whole into its compass. But between the pamphlet and the book there is one important difference, best indicated by Nin herself when she recalls the early work in her "Introduction": "My main theme was that one could find reality only by discarding realism," she remembers. But then she goes on to add, "I was speaking of psychological reality to an audience conditioned to representative social realism" (3). In view of the multiple ways in which one could interpret the key terms, the qualification is most necessary, a fact which Nin seems to have realized. And this constitutes the basic difference between the early and recent criticism—a greater precision with respect to critical terms and an attempt to clarify misunderstandings that have arisen from the early loose terminology. Usually it is only a qualifying word that does the job: "This emotional reality which underlies superficial incidents is the keynote of my fiction" (47); "It is to reach a greater *reality* (authenticity) that I abandoned realism" (45). But even a single adjective provides direction, as these examples indicate. In similar fashion she is now more careful in her attacks on the realists, seeming to be aware on the one hand that simply to denigrate them is not to prove a point and on the other that to condemn them outright is to damage her own cause, which is a belief in the poetic fusion of two extremes. Consequently, the tone of absolutism is replaced by one of relativism: "Many of those relationships so carefully documented by the realists are untrue to the deeper ones running beneath like an underground river . . ." (45). Formerly she used "intuition" as an irrefutable and final silencing word; now she is not only careful to define it but she also allows for its misuse:

> Even as a child I had an unusual awareness of what people felt. I had intuition about what went on behind appearances, and I trusted it and spoke out, as most children do, on the basis of that. Later I developed this intuition and gave it a sounder basis by the study of psychoanalysis. . . .
> In Webster's *New Twentieth Century Dictionary* we find this definition of intuition: "To know instinctively; to acquire knowledge by direct perception or comprehension. Perceived by the mind immediately without the intervention of argument or testimoney, having the power of discovering truth without reasoning."
> Intuition can be fallacious or accurate according to how often it is checked against reality and developed. (44-45)

The use of Webster as her authority may indicate an ironic condescension; nevertheless, the work as a whole creates the impression that she is attempting to make herself clearly understood. As we stated in the opening chapter of this study, when working with her early critical work it is necessary to provide a preliminary explanation of her terms before one can relate them to her practice; *The Novel of the Future* would eliminate that need did it not confirm its necessity.

"A SPADE IS A SPADE IS A SPADE IS A SPADE" (11) is Nin's headline for a section of her work which deals with the way in which extreme realism leads inevitably to its opposite. But by combining the mottoes of the reportage and the automatic writing schools she cleverly puts her finger on the major weakness of both—lack of discrimination. And this in turn points to the second area in which *The Novel of the Future* constitutes a revaluation of her earlier thought. In her youthful exuberance over the value of the unconscious, Nin was prone to forget to stress that it was essentially as material that this extra dimension was important and that artistry earned its way only through craft. Possibly because this led many of her reviewers to classify her as a "dreamer," possibly because she herself recognized the problem, in *The Novel of the Future* she repeatedly draws distinctions between the experience itself and the artistic reconstruction, between the poetic and the common response to the unconscious, between the artificial and the organic use of the dream. "Most fiction writers use dreams decoratively," she observes (6); the poetic writer is the one who retains their reality—not by a literal transcription of the unconscious but by shaping his perceptions through the medium of the symbol. Earlier she would have championed Gertrude Stein's method, perhaps; now she realizes that "the dream had to be expanded, recreated, could not be told literally for then it became as flat and one-dimensional as representational realism" (118). Form, not formlessness, then, is the distinguishing feature of the true poet of the interior. The unconscious rises in the artist as in all men, but the "discipline and form of an artist's work are set in the same system to prevent flooding. The amateur drowns" (7). Conversely, "Any artificial imitation of the unconscious can be easily detected. It is absurd and meaningless, it is chaotic and grotesque. The images are unrelated. They do not lead anywhere" (7). Unlike the day-dreamer, the organic writer exercises rather than surrenders control: "There is no doubt that the act of creation is very similar to the act of dreaming. The difference is that it includes an activity which has been difficult to analyse. It is not only the power to summon an image, but the power to compose with this image" (11). Unlike the neurotic, the artist creates not to express his frustrations but to communicate his convictions: "That is the difference between the paintings of the insane and of the artists: not only the talent, training, and gift are different, but the art itself is a form of control. Control, not suppression. The insane seek merely to decompress from too rigid a mold, and they explode. That is not the motivation of the artist. He is there to experience and describe experience" (139).[2] Generally speaking, none of this is new; long before this Coleridge, and long before Coleridge, aestheticians had argued the difference between the uncontrolled fancy and the shaping power of the imagination. Nor as far as Nin's general fictional practice is concerned is the emphasis upon artistic control a recent development; as far as her early critical statements, however, these positions do constitute something of a revaluation.

In addition to replacing "dream" with the qualified phrase, "directed dream" (32), *The Novel of the Future* also demonstrates Nin's attempt to be more precise with respect to that key word itself. "It is interesting to return to the original definition of a word we use too often and too carelessly" she writes in Emersonian fashion at the beginning of chapter one, pointing I suggest as much to her early self as to her unsympathetic critics.

The definition of a dream is: ideas and images in the mind *not under the command of reason*. It is not necessarily an image or an idea that we have during sleep. It is merely an idea or image which escapes the control of reasoning or logical or rational mind. So that dream may include reverie, imagination, day-dreaming, the visions and hallucinations under the influence of drugs—any experience which emerges from the realm of the

---

[2] For one of the promulgators of the theory Nin is attempting to refute see Simon O. Lesser, "The Functions of Form," *Fiction and the Unconscious* (New York, 1962), pp. 121-144.

subconscious. These various classifications are merely ways to describe different states or levels of consciousness. (5)

In a similar way she attempts to give a larger meaning to that other key word in her vocabulary, "neurosis": "For me neurosis is the contemporary expression of romanticism, where the ideal wish was unfulfillable and ended in withdrawal" (35). To the psychoanalytic critic, Nin's return to the broader and ancient meanings of such terms will seem only retrograde; to the literary critic it is the type of comment that redeems her earlier clinical bent, and encourages him, should it be necessary, to go back to her fiction and to approach it with traditional psychological rather than with modern psychoanalytic tools. Throughout *The Novel of the Future* Nin's concern is as always to emphasize her departure from the conventional mode of fiction, but now her explanations point as much to ancient practice as to a futuristic mode:[3]

> With my habit of going backstage always, I did not find that the drama lay in tragic incidents of a person's life, but in the hidden motivations which lay behind these incidents, the "interior fatality". . . . This meant finding the original wish by examining early dreams and fantasies, their progression and withering. . . . This is a different position from most novels which accept the influence of environment, outer pressures, the effect of incidents and accidents caused by society, history, etc. The tensions I set up (drama) were the tension between potential and fulfillment, outer and inner forces of destiny, outer and inner pressures. For this I could not be content with registering *action* without reflecting on how this action came about.
>
> Therefore my characters experience and reflect, experience and analyze simultaneously. So that the progression or movement may be a further degree of awareness which, for me, is the pivot of dramatic development. (56-57)

For Aristotle, also, anagnorisis is the pivot of drama, and character development the noblest action. In her early critical theory Nin described her fiction as "dramas of the unconscious"; in *The Novel of the Future* she employs a less medical, more poetic term—"psychodrama" (19); her fiction, from first to last we have labelled *psychomachia*.[4]

The Novel of the Future, in short, is Nin the critic coming to terms with Nin the artist. At the outset of her career she seemed to feel, like many

---

[3] Out of context, Nin's attempt to restore the original meaning of novel, i.e., *novella:* "new"(25), "the never-before-experienced"(90), would seem to contradict this interpretation. In context, however, it is obvious that she is using "new" in a relative sense and as the opposite to a superficial social experience. The feeling of love might be new to one raised on the concept of chemisms and the code of courtship.

[4] As a point of interest, I might mention that I chose *psychomachia* as the term most descriptive of Nin's type of drama before I discovered her remarkably similar term in *The Novel of the Future.*

psychoanalytic critics today,[5] that the psychoanalytic approach was not just another but *the* approach to literature; initially she appeared to be content with the single psychological meaning of ego. Now she insists upon the traditional three: "The philosophical definition: 'The entire man considered as a union of soul and body.' The metaphysical definition: 'The conscious and permanent subject of all experience.' The psychological definition: 'The self, whether considered as an organization of systems or mental states, or as the consciousness of the individual's distinction from other selves, and so as contrasted with an alter or alter ego' " (72-73).

In "The Writer and the Symbols" Anaïs Nin makes a list of those she considers the "heroes of the unconscious": "Freud, Proust and Joyce, Kafka, Djuna Barnes, etc."[6] In *The Novel of the Future* the list remains the same, although generally speaking, the order has been changed. Now it is the artist rather than the psychoanalyst that is given the leading role. This is not to say that in her early work she slighted the poet but that frequently her writing rang a jargonish and adolescent note announcing the literary advent of psychoanalysis; then her emphasis was upon the fact that literature was behind the times, that is, psychoanalytic discoveries. In *The Novel of the Future* the change in emphasis is evident in two typical kinds of comments. First, her continual comparison of the psychoanalytic writer to the ancient shaman: "In the old collective culture there was always room for the dreamer, the one who dreamed for the villagers, the one who interpreted dreams, omens, and myths, told tales, and preserved the history, ballads, and myths of the clan" (17). Instead of doing something radical, then, the modern writer is trying to recapture something that has been lost. Man's "nocturnal life is a mythological replica of and a key to his actions by day" (32), she writes, moving closer to Jung and towards the archetypal concept of art. Second, her tendency now is to give the scientist the task of proving what the poet has discovered: "This fascinating underworld of symbolic act has always been known to the poets. It was Freud who complained that every time he made a discovery he found some poet who had been there before him" (11). Or again, after observing the unannounced manner in which writers such as Kafka and Lautréamont descend into the unconscious, she explains, "Because their contention is that they are not separate, that we actually live by superimpositions of conscious and unconscious. Freud proved this scientifically. The artist knew it all the time" (121). Rightly, I think, one might detect in some of these comments a small undercurrent of nostalgia best explained in terms of her early partisanship; emotionally it is hard to admit even after many years that the manifesto is a characteristic of the "twenties." To accept the "new not new" is not easy when one began as an

---

    [5] See, for example, Norman N. Holland, *The Dynamics of Literary Response* (New York, 1968).

    [6] "The Writer and the Symbols," p. 40.

iconoclast. And in this respect one might even describe the expansions and retentions of *The Novel of the Future* as an attempt to salvage the youthful credo by giving it a traditional authority. For when it is a question of Nin, the young artist, *versus* a modern psychoanalyst, it is unequivocally the artist who is given priority: "Long before this [Dr. R. D. Laing's *Politics of Experience*] I had felt that this paring away was the role of the novelist . . ." (113). To some this will appear as the height of egotism, to others a most forgiveable weakness.

A final way of suggesting that in *The Novel of the Future* Nin is attempting to correct the negative aspects of her youthful manifesto is to consider her attitude toward her role as an innovator. The reader of her early critical statements could be excused, I think, for concluding that she saw herself as avant-garde in literary fashion. Not so the reader of the later work, or at least to a lesser degree: "In Paris, in the thirties, many writers around me were breaking the molds of the conventional novel and experimentation was encouraged" (1). That this is the second sentence of her "Introduction," indicates her awareness of its importance. Of equal importance is that despite her explanation of the difference occasioned by the move to America, she retains the plural: "In France we felt a part of a pioneering group, but in America we found ourselves isolated and in the minority" (1). Nor is the group sense merely a token gesture, since in *The Novel of the Future* she no longer relies only upon her own theory and practice but quotes extensively from others of the minority group, artists and theorists.

A similar mature understanding of the relation between tradition and the individual is apparent in her comments about writers who have influenced her. Through the use of the word "affinity" (57) she reinforces her initial concept of influence as a meeting of like minds rather than as the mechanical operation of one upon the other, but her emphasis now is upon admitting that one has forerunners:

> It is not a bad sign for a young writer to choose a model, for if this choice is genuine, it indicates an affinity and helps the young writer to find where he stands. I find young writers today too eager to disclaim any influences, to pay homage to those who helped them set their course, as if ashamed of their literary parents. I have no desire to claim that as a writer I was born in a cabbage patch. I owe my formative roots to D. H. Lawrence, Marcel Proust, Djuna Barnes, and the novels of Jean Giraudoux and Pierre Jean Jouve. I was influenced by Rimbaud and the surrealists. (117)

Of course, in admitting her own literary forebears she is also reminding modern literary children of their indebtedness to her. And this leads directly to the second general value of *The Novel of the Future*. For as much as it involves Nin's attempt to revaluate her youthful manifesto, it also is concerned with accommodating her theories to a modern youth and a somewhat changed world. A convenient link between these two central features is Nin's explanation of the necessity of the dream: *"Dreaming is indispensable to man.* Man has to learn to live *outside* and *beyond* history as well as in it, or he will be swept like hysterical sheep into its errors. . . . He needs a spiritual island where he can renew his strength, his shattered values, his traumatized emotions, his disintegrated faiths. It is the lack of such laboratories of the psyche which brings despair, pessimism, hysteria" (13). Echoing as it does, Mircea Eliade's philosophical diagnosis of the cause of modern man's anxiety it provides a most acceptable basis for her a-historical concept of fiction and also for her theory that the major problems of the modern world are a consequence of the absence of such a literature because of the realistic mode. According to Eliade, "The chief difference between the man of the archaic and traditional societies and the man of the modern societies with their strong imprint of Judaeo-Christianity lies in the fact that the former feels himself indissolubly connected with the Cosmos and the cosmic rhythms, whereas the latter insists that he is connected only with History."[7] Nin might say "unconscious" instead of "cosmic"; that is the only essential difference.

To Anaïs Nin, the taking of drugs is, like the absence of healthy sexual relations in the thirties, a symptom of a cultural neurosis, of a sick society. Like the earlier, this symptom is indicative of a dissociation from nature, from elemental and enduring values; like the earlier, it is a consequence of the substitution of a scientific notion of realism for the poetic concept of reality:

> For a long time in our utilitarian culture the dream was considered an escape, literature of imagination and experiment an escape. The young could only find a way out of such *rigidities* by extreme and dangerous methods. . . . We brainwashed the young as to what constitutes reality. The young are not seeking escape but expansion. . . .
>
> Every flight of fantasy has been condemned as a departure from reality. It was only logical that the young should turn to a synthetic way of reaching the world of the unconscious which was sealed off to them. (16-17)

It is not because the young have no values but because they sense an absence of values in the world that they turn to drugs according to Nin; "When we are amazed at the passivity, or the lack of inner resources, of some of the young, and their inertia, and their alienation, we never connect this with the positive denial of transient values in favor of more enduring ones" (68). But while she is thus totally sympathetic toward the problem, Nin in no way lauds the practice! "Drugs, by shutting out the external world, revived the faculty to dream, but this faculty is not a mere filmstrip to be looked at passively. It has two creative functions: one to keep the psyche alive in its

---

[7] Mircea Eliade, *Cosmos and History,* translated from the French by Willard R. Trask (New York, 1959), p. vii.

proper language (images and feelings); the other nourishes creation" (15). "The second faculty, the faculty of active creation, is what is missing from the use of drugs. Drugs induce passivity. Passivity, like the passivity of India induced by religion, is destructive both to human life and to art" (11).

Nor in making these judgments does she act as the arm-chair philosopher. She describes at length her own experience with LSD in order to "see if the world I described in my poetry resembled the world of LSD," and comes to the conclusion that it does but in a negative rather than in a positive way, "in a way that would ultimately consume or unbalance a human being" (89). Or again, she introduces the example of the French writer, Henri Michaux, who told her that he took drugs "at intervals of a year or two," and spent the intervening time struggling to define the experience (96). Finally, as of Michaux, she concludes that "Alan Watts is one of the best writers on psychic states, ecstasies, and mystical experiences, which may be due also to his literary discipline in writing about religions long before he became interested in the mystical states induced by LSD" (96). Conversely, "When a nonartist attempts to describe dreams, visions, hallucinations in a film such as *The Trip*, the absence of artistic means can only create vulgarity and garishness" (97). Her argument against drugs, in short, is similar to her argument against automatic writing and the extremes of surrealism.

Her solution to the drug problem consequently is two fold. First, only those who are emotionally stable and artistically mature should experiment: "The only one who can allow his unconscious to be free is the one who can understand its meaning and control its destructive aspects" (89). This is not restriction of but confrontation with the problem; it is the suppression of the traffic, like all suppressions, that occasions revolt; it is the placing of the materials in the proper hands that is the answer. Second, since the "young would have no need of drugs if they had been educated in the life of the senses and emotions through art" (16), "a good substitute for drugs would be the artist's vision" (89). "Art has through the ages given people their heightened sense of life, given them the key to its meaning" (16). Social controls merely compound the problem since they are its cause; art alone is capable of answering the need without adding to it, since it alone can contain the non-rational without either succumbing to it or suppressing it.

In addition to the drug culture, realism has given rise to two equally unhealthy features of modern life. Because of his empirical orientation, modern man believes that the world he sees is objectively real, whereas the truth lies in quite an opposite epistemology. "We carefully observe and watch the happenings of the entire world without realizing that they are projections of our inner selves. What we are watching outside is a representation, a projection of our inner world into the universal" (29). Consequently, there is no such thing as a detached observer; "The only objectivity we can reach is achieved, first of all, by an examination of our *self* as lens, as camera, as recorder, as mirror" (36). And it is this refusal to accept the subjectivity of perception that leads to the conclusion that the world is "completely insane, absurd, or else ourselves insane or meaningless" (29). Similarly, because of his rationalistic orientation, modern man believes that what cannot be scientifically verified and consciously apprehended does not exist, and this has "produced a kind of self-expression that spills over with a great mass of physical details to divert one from touching upon the truly significant experience. The result is overdensity, and a prestidigitation which eliminates the deeper meaning. This in turn leads to a theory that life has no meaning, is absurd, irrational" (43). With his mechanical and logical eyes, man discovers a nonrational world, and concludes that it is "absurd to treat such events with rational logic" (171). But instead of blaming his own mode of perception and attempting to adjust it, he becomes passive and fatalistic; "people prefer to accept the notion of the absurd rather than to search for the meaning . . ." (171). To Nin, in short, realism is the father of the absurd element in the philosophy of existentialism; to her it is not the supremely heroic stance but a cultural symptom, a defense mechanism: "The most powerful of literary movements, which I call 'resistantialism,' consists of those who are afraid of going inside, who have a fear of intimacy or contact with human beings. They feel such proximity will cloud their insight or involve their feelings. They defend themselves against feeling with irony and clowning" (168). It is not the world that is absurd in the modern philosophical sense, but the man who sees it as such, in the old original sense; "The metaphysical concept that our life has a meaning is deeper than that reached by the materialist that the world is absurd and meaningless (Camus). The sense of emptiness came from accepting only what we see and not what lies beyond appearances. What we see is altered by what we feel" (185). If we are a sad society, the fault lies not in the stars but in our telescopes: "The pessimism which has colored present writing would not exist if men had not turned their backs on the science of human nature in favor of all the other sciences. . . . It is also strange that, just as we were about to discover our power to change destiny, we surfaced to an almost completely external world where the human being is more than ever in danger of annihilation, not from bombs, but from passivity" (192). Like the taking of drugs, the philosophy of the absurd is a sign of the times; both are symptoms of something that has gone wrong and both can be cured only by going back to the source of the problem, not by inventing a new "way out" (16).

"The cult of ugliness so apparent in our novels is another misinterpretation of reality," according to Anaïs Nin:

> Because so many of our writers were born in ugly environments, in monstrous poverty and humiliation, they continue to assert that this is the natural environment, reality, and that beauty is artifice. Why should the natural state be ugliness? Natural to whom? We may be born in ugliness,

but the natural consequences should be a thirst for its opposite. To mistake ugliness for reality is one of the frauds of the realistic school. (197)

Instead of a healthy honesty, the writer who dwells on the sordid reveals a perverted sense of values; instead of a seer or a saviour, he is a masochist and a sadist. "The *cult of ugliness* is distinct from the acceptance that there is ugliness, just as taking pleasure in cruelty is distinct from the acceptance that there is cruelty in the world" (165). Like all realists, the bleak writer is unable to recognize the subjectivity of his vision and lacks the a-temporal perspective of the genuine artist; "an obsession with ugliness lies ultimately in the writer's vision of the world, and when the writer loses his perspective and balance, he adds to the ugliness" (165). Just as it is not bombs but passivity that threaten the annihilation of the race, it is not the pollution of the air by smoke but "the pollution of humanity by hate" that should be our immediate concern. The polluter of our environment is not the tin can and the billboard but the person who perpetuates them in art: "When we decided to believe only what was visible, we lost the faculty for apprehending what might be. Out of such a distorted view of *what is* came the monstrosities of pop art" (174). Instead of being a progressive mode, like the cult of absurdity or the taking of drugs the non-art movement is retrogressive, escapist and childish. "Accepting what is (a complete service station in a museum, Campbell's Soup cartons and billboards in our living room) is an act of passivity, an act of resignation, of impotence, lack of invention and transformation, also an inability to discard *what is* and create *what might be*" (174). To Nin, such artists are not rebels but slaves, or rather not artists at all but imitators, realists. When the true artist writes about the ugly he transforms it; "Those who stay in their hostile and hated environment are the neurotics who are traumatized and paralyzed. . . ." (197). The artist destroys in order to create, but the pseudoartist destroys because he cannot create. To her, the most interesting thing about *In Cold Blood* is its revelation of Capote's "personal, psychological attraction" to such a story (79) while "a loss of appetite for life" is the cause of Burroughs' *Naked Lunch* (198).

But pop and anti-art could not flourish unless there was an ideology to sustain them. Empiricism and realism provide the parentage, but for them to persist there must be a cultural sanction. America, according to Anaïs Nin, provides the necessary climate: "Our American culture decided at one point to trust the 'objective' vision of many against the one, the 'subjective'" (78). Instead of the raising of all men to the level of artists, America has reduced the artist to the quality of the common man. It had to, since by its constitution all men are equal and by its cultural heritage the hero is the self-made man. Unfortunately, "our admiration of the self-made man turned perversely into admiration of the unskilled, the amateur, the imperfect, the childish, the unformed, immature, incomplete, with a prejudice against the virtuoso, the original, inventive, talented individual" (95). Similarly, the ideal of democracy has naturally led to the "loss of identity," and paradoxically explains why "the theme of alienation has been so obsessive in the American novel" (36). Together, the two culminate in contemporary American writing, according to Nin best exemplified by Bowles' *The Sheltering Sky* and Albee's *The Zoo Story*, works in which an act of violence demonstates the extreme to which the American (tough) hero will and must go in order to relate to another. America, then, is the cultural seed-bed of the realistic mode of life and the epitome of the sickness it produces.

> Madmen who lose contact with reality usually regress to their primitive animal behavior and use primitive animal language. Some of our writers favor lavatory writing, graffiti, gutter language, army barracks or clinical expressions. At first this seemed the inevitable consequence of the age of the common man, of uneducated writers, of proletarian social realism and the naturalistic novel. But now I see another aspect of it. It may well be a sign of neurotic lack of sense of reality, that is, an effort to make one's experience real by use of brutal expressions, to shock one's self into feeling by the senses, again a perversion born of puritanism. To write aesthetically or emotionally about sensuality was *not real*. To be real, language must be violent, vulgar, and crude. (100)

And the final proof of its neuroticism is that while it complains of its condition, it clings tenaciously to it, like a neurotic to his symptom: "We protest against the violence, but we do not read the non-violent writers. We protest against the absence of contact, but we do not read the writers who deal with relationships and not with nonrelationships or antirelationships" (173).

And it is in this context that Anaïs Nin introduces the case of the woman writer in America, and the contrast between Europe and America.

> The man who has made the definitive conquest of nature, the American man, is the one most afraid of woman as *nature*, of the feminine in himself. The American created a monolithic image of maleness which is a caricature of maleness, an exaggeration of maleness (no sensitivity, only toughness, logic, factualness). The European did not achieve such a domination of nature but did not feel totally estranged from it and thus he lives more comfortably in a state of friendship with woman and feminine nature. (39)

Europe, to her, is symbolic of "an even balance between its naturalistic writers and its imaginative writers, between its classical writers and its innovators" (172). She is not making a political or personal but a poetic comment. What she says concerning woman, similarly must not be taken literally. It is less specifically female writers than the sensitivity associated with them that she argues for, since she includes in her argument a number of men: "The man who proceeds like a woman, in leaps, is the artist, the creative scientist, and the inventor" (39). Conversely, it is not man, but the tough writer against whom she takes arms, the male critic who out of hand condemns women writers, and men like them, as "small subjective and personal" (38). "There was no declaration of war between the sexes in my work," she states explicitly. "In a true relationship there is no taking sides, no feminine claims in opposition to masculine claims, no reproaches at all. There is an effort to confront together what interferes with genuine fusions" (76). To Nin, woman needs man as much as he needs her, and any attempt at independence is both self-destructive and sad; when man attempts it he becomes the rootless American, when woman attempts it she is likely to become Marguerite Young's "Cousin Hannah, the suffragette. She spent her life trying to overthrow man, but when she died, they found forty trunks filled with wedding dresses" (186). In short, to Nin woman's attempt to establish her identity through political or social movements is basically a selling out to the realists—a reliance upon purely external means. For both woman and man, "The sexual revolution, by itself and alone, is not going to put an end to loneliness or alienation" (198). First must come an understanding of one's self and one's natural relationship to others. The creative personality, male or female, "never resigns itself to anything. That is the deepest meaning of rebellion, not the wearing of different clothes, haircuts or adopting other cultures" (197).

To the question posited at the outset of this chapter, then, one must answer no and yes. As far as her basic theory of the difference between realism and reality is concerned she has not changed. As far as her early "manifesto" is concerned, however, there are two important changes: first, she has attempted to give clarity and authority to her youthful announcements; and second, she has attempted to demonstrate the truth of her perceptions by showing that they apply as much to the present as to the original time of writing. Thus one way to sum up is with the conclusion Anaïs Nin herself chooses for *The Novel of the Future*—a comment on the relevance of her theory of realism and reality—but made by another:

"The main problems of modern art have not changed since the nineteenth century. Realism or some form of anti-realism—this is still the question at the centre of the artist's choice of method. From Zola to William Burroughs, how to deal with an experience grown increasingly monstrous and fantastic remains the heart of the matter." (200)

VIII

☆ ☆ ☆ ☆ ☆

My Father, My World, My Children, My Dreams

Anaïs Nin herself provides the best introduction to the respective dimensions of her *Diary* when in the early pages of the first volume she invites the reader to

> Enter this laboratory of the soul where incidents are refracted into a diary, dissected to prove that everyone of us carries a deforming mirror where he sees himself too small or too large, too fat or too thin. . . . Enter here where one discovers that destiny can be directed, that one does not need to remain in bondage to the first wax imprint made on childhood sensibilities. One need not be branded by the first pattern. Once the deforming mirror is smashed, there is a possibility of wholeness, there is a possibility of joy. (I, 105)

Since it is concerned with actual incidents, the *Diary* does have a historical dimension; since these incidents are dissected in order to reveal their poetic and philosophical potential, the *Diary* does have a critical aspect; since these incidents are refracted rather than merely reflected, the *Diary* is also an artistic work. And it is this combination of elements that makes it the comprehensive example of its nominal class, which generally includes the factual records of a Pepys, the literary notebooks of a James, and the art of introspection of a Proust.

The general theme of the *Diary,* as this passage also implies, is the negative consequences of the mirror approach to life and art and of the need and the possibility of replacing such a static and deterministic view with a positive and organic one. The symbolic "first pattern" has philosophical and artistic as well as psychological referents, as a brief thematic survey of this "pilgrim's progress of the artist" (*Novel,* 146) will demonstrate. The *Diary* began as a letter by Nin, the child, to the father who had without apparent reason left her. Thus initially, the journal was, like a primitive ritual, a concrete attempt to maintain contact with the invisible and to confront the inexplicable. When the continued absence led to a weakening of faith in the imminence of a reunion, the writing of the journal become confessional and the *Diary* the outlet for questions directed outward but with answers discovered inward. This situation, in turn, gave the *Diary* a new and romantic function: to preserve the personal memory by creating the literary image and to protect this image by keeping it secret. Then the father appears, and the crucial confrontation takes place, the meeting of the ideal and the actual, the stage where typically occurs disillusionment. But after moments of despair and moments of obstinate self-delusion, the diarist comes to two awarenesses; first, that her ideal was one no human being could fulfill, and second, that ironically the reason her father appeared to have failed was that he was trying to live according to a similar ideal. But instead of burning her books, she redirects her search; instead of rejecting the ideal in favor of the realistic she becomes a transcendentalist and an artist:

> I do not think I am looking for a man, but for a God. I am beginning to feel a void which must be the absence of God. I have called for a father, a guide, a leader, a protector, a friend, a lover, but I still miss something: it must be God. But I want a god in the flesh, not an abstraction, an incarnated god, with strength, two arms, and a sex.
>
> *Perhaps I have loved the artist because creation is the nearest we come to divinity.* (I, 262-263, emphasis mine)

It is in this symbolic sense that the *Diary* involves a search for the father—a psychological search for a balanced personality, a philosophical search for an integrating perspective, an aesthetic search for the epiphanic art form. And it is for this reason that the search never ends, that the pattern we have described is a thematic one repeated with variations throughout all of the volumes. What makes the *Diary* profound and universal is not the isolated comment but the archetypal nature of the quest; and what gives the work its artistic form is its theme.

"The hero of this book may be the soul, but it is an odyssey from the inner to the outer world," writes Nin shortly after describing her "laboratory" (I, 107). On the one hand this movement may be traced in chronological fashion by examining the controlling subject of each of the four respective volumes so far published. On the other hand this odyssey may be considered in terms of the movement from the private journal to the public works. Since the latter movement both precedes and forms a basis for the former, it is this personal aspect of realism and reality that we should examine first.

In the *Diary*, however, Nin's comments on the relative merits of the journal and the fiction reflect the psychological conflict itself and consequently if not considered in context they may appear to be contradictory. Thus instead of approaching the *Diary* itself it will be helpful to consider what she has to say in a less immediate and more objective situation, especially since two chapters in *The Novel of the Future* seem specifically designed for this purpose. "The Genesis of the Diary" begins with the unequivocal statement: "The writing of a diary has both its negative and its positive aspects" (*Novel,* 142); and the first of the negative aspects which she mentions is that it leads one to neglect "formal works, novels, or stories" (142). The second unfortunate aspect is the converse; the diary can be an escapist form; it can be "limited, trivial, narrow in its range," in which case "it is valueless" (145). Of passing interest for the present purposes except for the metaphor is the third reason: "The diarist is a camera" (150) and consequently reflects the quality of the lens as much as he captures the essence of the object. And this leads to the last and most important reason, the diary as a form of writing is limited to the immediate focus of the diarist. In the chapter entitled "Diary Versus Fiction," Nin states the problem clearly: "The necessity for fiction . . . was not only a need of the imagination but an answer to the limitations placed on portrayal of others" (155). Because diary writing is a historical form it does not answer to the aspirations of the genuine artist whose goal is creation rather than reflection.

Paradoxically, but significantly, the positive aspects of writing a diary lead ultimately in this same direction, for the central reason she advances for the diary is the limitations of fiction, that is fiction in the forms it traditionally takes. "Most of us, when beginning to write, create a persona as a defense from the world" (147). This *"fear of the world,"* in turn results in guarded and stilted writing. Because the diary is not meant for public perusal, then, it enables the young writer to bypass "all the inhibiting factors" (144), and consequently to write more honestly. Secondly, the diary functions as a necessary and informal discipline: "Keeping a notebook also taught me that to achieve perfection while attaining naturalness it is important to write a great deal, to write fluently rather than revise over and over again" (147). To Nin, the writer should not pen his *magnum opus* and then revise it to death but rather practice exhaustively in preparation for the masterpiece. In addition to teaching good technique the keeping of a diary also trains the writer to recognize the bad and the reasons for it. In the first place, keeping a diary makes one aware of life's continual changes and thus makes one realize that it is the "tale without beginning or end which encloses all things" (159), not the story with a pat beginning, middle, and end that is the appropriate artistic form. Secondly, "The diary also teaches that it is in the moments of emotional crisis that human beings reveal themselves most accurately" (159), and that consequently one such brief incident tells more and tells better than the tome concerned with objective description. The positive value of the diary, then, is that it allows the writer to capture the "living essence" whereas fiction traditionally results in its death. The positive value of the diary is its possible organicism, its garden dimensions: "Here I was, back to the watching of the flower's roots, watching its growth" (145).

These, then, are the two sides to the debate between the fiction and the journals, but it is not in a deadlock that the issue remains. Initially, Nin tells us, she saw the two as conflicting modes, and the literary situation being what it was, she at that time championed the diary (156). But then she came to the realization that the two could coexist harmoniously because the solution was to revivify the novel, not to announce its obituary (155–156). "The diary, then, was where I checked my realities and illusions, made my

99

experiments, noted progress or its opposite. It was the laboratory!" (157).
"In the diary I documented a visit to the ragpickers. In the story I showed
how it could be more than that" (158). The purpose of fiction now becomes
"symbolization, the creation of myth" (158); the purpose of the diary, to
provide the novelist with "living food."

> Which does not mean that all my fiction is autobiographical, nor does it
> mean as some believe, that I am all the women in my novels (it would be
> pleasant in one life to be so many women!). It simply means that the
> psychological reality of each character had been taken first from a living
> heart. Whether or not the transplant was successful, I leave to critics. It is
> a pity that to achieve an evaluation, the novels have to undergo dissection.
> (146)

And according to Nin, only "an uncreative person" would engage in such
"sleuthing" (157), would futilely attempt mechanically to undo what the
writer had artistically done.

"Why did I not remain merely a diarist?" she asks, and then answers,
"Because there was a world beyond the personal which could be handled
through art form, through fiction" (161). And further explaining the development of her art, "Why did I not stay within *House of Incest* and write
only prose poems, dreamed material such as *Les chants de Maldoror?*" she
asks. "Because my drive was stated by Jung: *proceed from the dream outward*. I took this as relating dream and life, internal and external worlds,
the secrets and persona of the self. Appearance and reality, illusion and
reality" (161). According to *The Novel of the Future,* then, initially the
Diary came first but ultimately the fiction, and today the tables have turned
even further: "By 1966 it was the experience of the novelist which helped
me to edit the *Diary*. It was the fiction writer who knew when the tempo
lagged, when details were trivial, when a description was a repetition. I
changed nothing essential, I only cut the extraneous, the overload" (164).

By way of turning from the personal to the more historical aspects
of Nin's odyssey from the inner to the outer, one should notice a final
explanation from *The Novel of the Future*. Her rationale in editing, she
suggests, was not whether a figure had become famous but whether or not
he was representative (*Novel,* 147-148). In the following discussion of the
controlling subject of each of the volumes of the *Diary* it is similarly repre-
sentativeness that is the guiding principle. The *Diary* is a rich and variegated
tapestry which it is not my intention to unravel, but there is, I think, a
single unbroken thread to be found, an Ariadne's thread whose strands are
realism and reality.

i

Volume one of the *Diary* begins when Anaïs Nin had completed her
first piece of formal writing, *D. H. Lawrence: An Unprofessional Study,*

and ends with her preparations to go to New York in order to practice analysis. The first half of the work focuses upon her relationship with Henry Miller, the second, her movement from René Allendy to Otto Rank. And it is the symbolic significance of these three men that gives the volume its central theme; Henry in literature and Allendy in psychoanalysis are representative of the realist approach to life; against the former Nin pits her own poetic perceptions, against the latter she posits the poetic understanding of Rank.

The Lawrence book literally and metaphorically brought Anaïs Nin and Henry Miller together. But that they were approaching from opposite directions became obvious with the arrival of "the perpetually disguised woman," June (41). Both recognized in her a challenge to their literary powers and in their attempts to capture her essence in words began the struggle between them. "For Henry," she writes, "illusions and lies are synonymous. Art and illusion are lies. Embellishment. In this I feel remote from him, totally in disagreement with him" (18). Whereas Nin feels that it is exactly the mystery of the enigmatic that the writer must try to capture, Miller feels that the mystery must and can be exploded; he thinks that "If he annotates enough facts, he will finally possess the truth" (18), that if he plays mechanical detective long enough he will arrive at the formula. Part of his problem, according to Nin, is his approach and attitude, but as great a part is his language: "Henry feels that he has not got June in his novel. There is one world closed to him. It is the oblique, indirect world of subtle emotions and ecstasies, those which do not taken a physical form, a plain physical act. He said he would never stop banging his head against it. I said, 'There are some things one cannot seize by realism, but by poetry. It is a matter of language'" (55). Miller's problem, then, the problem of all realists, is that he attempts a literal transcription of emotion instead of a symbolic translation (151).

A concrete and timely example from the *Diary* of the difference between the poet and the realist is their respective attitudes towards lesbianism. The latter takes the situation at face value and introduces circumstantial evidence: if two women enjoy each other it must be a physical thing. The poet looks at the context and beneath the appearances; "'If there is an explanation of the mystery, it is this: the love between women is a refuge and an escape into harmony and narcissism in place of conflict. Two women do not judge each other. They form an alliance. It is, in a way, self-love'" (41). The artist seeks the reason for one's actions; the materialist judges by appearances.

To Leon Edel, Nin's attempts to make peace between Miller and June reflect "a troubled pre-adolescent pursuing a dream of reuniting her parents" through these substitute figures.[1] However true that may be it is far from complete. A more profitable and substantial way of viewing the situation is to consider Miller and June as symbolic of the two literary extremes that Nin is attempting to reconcile: "They must have been drawn together by his need to expose illusion, her need to create it. A satanic pact. One of them must triumph: the realist or the mythmaker" (18). Emotionally she is aligned with June, intellectually with Miller, and it is because she wants both that she cannot for long take either side: "I saw a new truth. . . . I am not vacillating between Henry and June, but between two truths I see with clarity. I believe in Henry as a human being, although I am fully aware of the literary monster. I believe in June, although I am fully aware of her destructive power" (134).

From the beginning of the *Diary,* then, Nin seems aware of the problem though not of the resolution: "Again and again I have entered realism, and found it arid, limited. Again and again I return to poetry. . . . But poetry took me away from life, and so I will have to live in Henry's world" (55). But Henry's world is one of realistic poetry, not of poetic realism, of Whitmanesque catalogues and surrealistic formlessness. Speaking of *House of Incest,* he advises her to " 'Elaborate! That is the only way out of those watertight abstractions of yours. Break through them, divest them of their mystery and allow them to flow.' " To which she answers, that perhaps some elaboration is needed but that Miller's request for flow reveals his misunderstanding of the relation between the practice and the poetic product born of it: "I think he does not understand that it is because I have a natural flow in the diary: what I produce outside is a distillation, the myth, the poem. The elaboration is here [in the *Diary*]. [*House of Incest*] is the gem made out of this natural outpouring. Shouldn't people prefer gems" (198).

Miller's appetite for the crude rather than the refined leads her to three considerations: first, that their relationship is "not just a personal one" but symbolic of the difference between "the aristocrat and the common man, the civilized and the primitive" (222). The union of the two is what she desires, but she fears that the future will bring the era of the latter: "The man of tomorrow will come from the people, will deny civilization. What will happen to that core of fury and bitterness" she wonders, when it will not be controlled by the artist's sense of value. To her, passionate and uninhibited writing is essential, but as the first not the last stage of creation; "I believe in impulse and naturalness, but followed by discipline in the cutting" (167). Pruning does not kill the plant but aids its growth; the unattended garden reverts to chaos.[2] Secondly, she begins to wonder whether the crudeness of

---

[1] Leon Edel, "Life Without Father," *Saturday Review* (May 7, 1966), p. 91. "Myopic Leon Edel," Nin calls him in *The Novel of the Future,* for adopting a literal and psychoanalytic approach to the *Diary* (*Novel,* p. 145).

[2] For this idea elaborated in a Miltonic setting, I refer you to a lecture by John J. Teunissen, in the series "Man and Cosmos," delivered on the Canadian Broadcasting Corporation, National Network, January 13, 1971.

Miller, the realists' obsession with the concrete, is a genuine reflection of a perspective or a defense mechanism: "Henry is a demon driven by curiosity, always pumping people. Henry is always pretending callousness. Is that an American disease? They are ashamed to show feeling" (92). "Does he satirize what he doesn't understand? Was it his way of conquering what eludes him?" (131). And finally, she considers whether environment is responsible for their difference in literary values: "His life. The lower depths, the underworld" (56), and hers a world of music, books, and artists. Is a person's outlook a predetermined thing; is man a blind mechanism with no control over his own development?

Because she sensed in herself the double attraction for the human actuality and the artistic possibility and because she wanted to create her own destiny rather than to accept the pattern shaped of circumstance Nin turned to psychoanalysis. She became interested in this branch of psychology, that is, not as a patient seeking medical aid but as a sensitive individual who wanted to know more about the nature of her duality in order to reconcile its respective claims: "I felt overwhelmed by reality. . . . I am living either in a dream or in pure sensuality. No intermediate life" (160). She had read of the French psychoanalyst, René Allendy, and of the German, Otto Rank. Fortunately she turned to the former first, fortunate because the experience enabled her to distinguish between psycho- and poetic-analysis, between the mechanist of the psyche and the explorer of the soul.

Allendy, in the first volume of the *Diary,* comes to be representative of the reductive direction of psychoanalysis, of the realist approach to the unconscious, and it is the artist's discovery of this limitation that is the central significance of this encounter. It was Allendy's belief in directed destiny that attracted her; it was his scientific application of the theory that repelled her. In the first place, one notices that his approach to her "case" is remarkably comparable to Miller's attempts to dissect June: "He questioned me relentlessly. He feels there is a secret. The theme of flight does not satisfy him. I feel that something in me escapes his definitions" (108). Like the realist, instead of admitting his limitations he imposes them: "Today I find flaws in Dr. Allendy's formulas. I am irritated by his quick categorizing of my dreams and feelings" (108). And that the irritation is an indication of the reductivism of the analysis and not the neurosis of the analyzed becomes clear when one discovers the direction in which he hopes to lead her, the average, the normal, the even social being: "Here I balk a little. If psychoanalysis is going to divest me of all decoration, costume, adornment, flavor, characteristic, then what will be left?" (199). He wants to reconcile her to herself which he assures her is a basically good and respectable human being: "This was the natural conclusion to the formation of my human self, to normalcy" (282) and that "conclusion" she writes "put an end to my faith in Allendy. Whatever magic I had been able to find in analysis, whatever beneficial influence, was defeated by the kind of Anaïs this naturalness was leading me into. Rather than enter this ordinary life, which was death to my imagination" she would choose to be neurotic. "Disease was, in this case, more inspiring and more fertile to poetry" (282).

The problem, in short, is that Nin is an artist and he is a scientist. When she confronts him with this argument, he revealingly denies it by saying that he has many artist friends and a sister-in-law who is a painter (131). And the final way in which the psychoanalyst reveals himself to be the medical realist is that, like Miller's reaction to June's relations to other women, he treats her admiration of her father literally rather than metaphorically. To him it can be reduced to psychological incest, the Electra complex (272). Like all scientists, he thinks that in discovering the skeleton, he had captured the essence; like the realist he thinks the object is the reality.

Because she had learned from his writings that "He had made a specialty of the 'artist' " Nin turns to Otto Rank (269), who immediately distinguishes himself from the Freudians: " 'I go beyond the psychoanalytical. Psycho-analysis emphasizes the resemblance between people; I emphasize the differences between people. They try to bring everybody to a certain normal level. I try to adapt each person to his own kind of universe. The creative instinct is apart' " (271). Thus whereas Allendy reduced her relation to her father to a "complex," Rank relates her situation to that of the "double" in the literature of Cervantes and Dostoevsky, on the one hand, and to the mythological records of the artist's struggle for independence, on the other. When she tells him that she feels like "a shattered mirror" he explores the symbolism of her description with her instead of labelling the feeling: " 'Why a mirror? A mirror for others? To reflect others, or yourself living behind a mirror and unable to touch real life?' " (273). When she tells him about the diary, he tells her about Scheherazade (277). Instead of trying to rid her of fantasy he encourages her imagination, instead of struggling to discover her "secret" with questions, he allows her to explain and encourages her to express herself in art. And most important of all for Nin's specific case, he explains the poetic approach to the unconscious and consequently why he has departed from orthodox practice: " 'I believe analysis has become the worst enemy of the soul'," because like all scientific disciplines, " 'It killed what it analyzed' " (277). This same murder of the living essence was what she had seen in the traditional novel and that had made her turn away from formal writing. Through Rank she discovers a new system of poetics.

Thus when she insists that Rank should not be confused with other psychoanalysts she is also explaining why her work should not be confused with that of other Freudian artists:

> He uses the same language, the same method, but he transcends the psychoanalytic theories and writes more as a philosopher, as a metaphysician.
>
> The axis of psychoanalysis is displaced by Rank, and the preoccupation becomes a metaphysical or creative one. It is this emphasis I want to make

clear, for a great popular confusion tends to classify all psychoanalysts more or less in the same pragmatic category: as doctors and not as seers, as healers and not as philosophers. Even though they deal with psychic illness, illness of the soul, the cure they offer is vaguely understood to be a sexual one. (297)

The public tone of this passage and the similarity in attitude to her comments in *The Novel of the Future* remind one that Nin was editing the *Diary* at the same time that she was writing the critical work. The revaluations we found in the critical work, in short, may have been occasioned by her renewed awareness of the difference between the scientific Allendy and the poetic Rank.

In volume one of the *Diary,* then, Anaïs Nin records her birth as an artist and also the birth of her own literary principles; it involves the symbolic rejection of the literal father and the quest for the incarnated one—neither man nor god, the real nor the ideal but the one in the other, the artist.

ii

The first forty pages of volume two of the *Diary* are concerned with Nin's experiences as a lay analyst in New York. While this might seem to be material which should conclude the first volume rather than open the second, when one examines the nature of this experience it becomes clear that the episode is properly positioned as an introduction to the central theme of the second volume, the question of the public responsibility of the artist.

In the first place, Nin learns from direct experience the general philosophical truth that is basic to her creative and critical writing, the fallacy of the objective and the converse significance of the intuitive and the personal. Rank explains and her patients demonstrate: "how little objectivity there is in man's thinking. Even in the most rational man, there is a fund of irrational motivations which are personal, and belong to his personal past, to his emotional traumas. So in the end, pure thought rarely exists in its abstract form, it is part of the experience and of the emotions" (19). Systems of all kinds, whether political or ideological, are not rational but rationalized constructions. The theoretician begins not with detached observation but with a personal bias which he disguises through generalization; the public minded citizen may be pure selfishness in disguise. The critic's concern with "the guilt tragedies in Dostoevsky" may reflect "his own guilts which he is unwilling to recognize or to name"; the politician's concern with "the hunger of China or India" may be an expression of "his own personal starvations. Man's language is that displacement from the personal to the impersonal, but this is another form of self-deception. The self in them is disguised, it is not absent as they believe" (25).

Secondly, through her practice, Nin acquires confirmation of her feeling concerning the relative merits of science and art insofar as humanity itself is the issue. Science may be able to accelerate biological development or rapidly to change the direction of vegetative growth, but the human being cannot be so quick-cured: "The patterns have deep roots and take time to change" (23). Further, to provide the patient with the answer to his problem is not to provide him with the solution; to make him intellectually aware is not to provide emotional direction. And it is just this emotional impulse that the modern is searching for: "Science may heal, but it is the poetic illumination of life which makes my patients fall in love with life, which makes them recover their appetite for it. I avoid labels and the hospital atmosphere" (23). But in avoiding these things, she is acting not as an analyst but as an artist, as she quickly realized.

Thus while it can be said that one of the reasons why she quit her practice was that she had little time for writing, better expression is that she recognized that she was an artist and that it was in this role that she could make her greatest contribution, that if the world had more genuine artists it would have less need for analysts, that the artist expended himself unwisely in public causes. For when she returned to Paris—and the Spanish Civil War—it is this argument that she expands against the call to political involvement.

To anticipate the charge that Nin adopted the philosophy of the politically detached artist as a way of excusing herself from active participation during the revolution, it may be well to notice that she advances her argument before the outbreak of violence, shortly after her return to Paris. "What makes people despair," she writes in June, 1935, "is that they try to find a universal meaning to the whole of life, and then end up by saying it is absurd, illogical, empty of meaning" (45). To her way of thinking, it is not from the comprehensive scheme but from the integrated individuals that collective happiness must come. One's best "contribution to the whole" is the perfection of one's self; not in the public cry for universal democracy but in the personal practice of sympathy does one demonstrate true humanity: "For example, I am not committed to any of the political movements, which I find full of fanaticism and injustice, but in the face of every human being, I act democratically and humanly." She will not make herself publically responsible for the fate of the world but "personally responsible for the fate of every human being who has come my way" (45). Allegiance to a political party more frequently supports the member than the cause.

And in 1936 and after, she continues to stick to these guns. Her opponent in this political aspect of the debate between realism and reality is Gonzalo, symbolic of "a type very prevalent in Europe at that time, caught between his political beliefs and his inability to act, to sacrifice himself, to discipline himself" (*Novel*, 148). Like the literary realist, the revolutionary is myopic and can focus only on the present and the apparent causes of the problem. When he urges her in the name of humanity to take a side she observes that politics are "based on economics, not humanitarianism" (92) and rhetorically wonders, "Was there ever a pure revolution" (278). Revolution is never for the good of all, she realizes, recalling that "the Inquisition tortured human beings who did not believe in Catholicism, and that [this] revolution will torture and is torturing all those who do not adhere fanatically to it" (278). Freedom for all is an absolute slogan with a relative significance. The revolutionary sees the victims of today, the visionary sees them the victimizers of tomorrow: "Someday, these same downtrodden workmen will become the tyrants, the same greedy inhuman 'bosses'" (188). It is a change of men not of roles. The anarchist argues that it is inequality that is the cause; the archetypalist argues that "injustice and cruelty are inherent in man" (223), that war is a modern form of ritual originating in the loss of the old. "The horrors of Spain. Who can cure man of cruelty? They have bullfights. But instead of a bull, it is a rebel . . ." (155). And if the loss of ritual is the cause then its restoration through art is the solution, and since realism is the literary cause, the proper revolution is against it: "The monster I have to kill every day is realism. The monster who attacks me every day is destruction. Out of these duels come transformation. I have to turn destruction into creation over and over again" (145).

The personality of the anarchist is comparable to that of the anti-artist: "Rebellions of all kinds attract to their activities weaklings who rebel because they cannot master, destroy because they cannot create. I fear that Gonzalo may be a part of that lamentable army, those who have always lived negatively" (272). Unlike the genuine revolutionary who views destruction as a means to creation, the malcontent uses such means to cloak his own inadequacies. Instead of accepting his personal limitations he blames an impersonal institution. "He says, 'The capitalistic world killed the artist in me'." And Nin replies, "He sees as coming from outside all that comes from inside. I know the artist in him must have been very weak to be defeated by this obstacle at all" (156). The times are always right for the artist because he is of no time, while the times are always out of joint for the pretenders. It is because like the realist he has no inside that he must clamor for external activity, it is because he has lost his sensitivity that he must relate to a cause with violence: "There are people who cannot change from the inner to the outer, who must be pushed from the outside. They are the ones who need revolutions. There are those who can rise above life, transform it, free themselves, and for these the revolution is not necessary" (321).

Like the realist who is unable to discriminate between the significant and the trivial and so includes everything, the rebel is unable to distinguish between the system and the abuse and so demands total annihilation. "'Curse all intellectual worlds. Literary worlds. Burn those books. . . .

The poor need bread. Did those books of yours solve the problems of the world?'" asks Gonzalo; to which Nin gently answers, "'Not all problems are economic'" (131). Convinced that it is books which keep her from becoming politically involved, Gonzalo "like a fanatical, like an Inquisitor," takes his metaphor literally and throws into the fire all the books within sight.[3] "When he had gone, it was dark. I rescued the books which had not caught fire," writes Nin symbolically; the works which are unable to be touched by the fury of the fanatic are those of "the great unrealists" (312).

Understandably the works most antagonistic to the militant realist are those by such men as Rank, since such psychoanalysis is "the great enemy of Marxism" (131). Whereas the former shouts that reform must come from without, the latter and Nin believe that the only lasting transformation is an inner and personal thing: "The only world I know without walls, injustices, monstrosities, is that of illusion and poetry. For me that is the only liberation" (310). But to conclude from such statements that "she cannot shed her basic political pessimism"[4] is sadly to misinterpret her attitude. It is because she is *for* the personal that she has no faith in the political, not the other way around; she does not "confess" that she has not taken sides in the Spanish Civil War, she explains why she believes in remaining above political entanglements. It is because she is archetypal in her attitude toward human nature, not because she is politically disillusioned that she writes, "Deep down, I feel nothing changes the nature of man" (154).

"And I asked myself if the artist who creates a world of beauty to sustain and transcend and transmute suffering is wiser than those who believe a revolution will remove the cause of suffering," Nin writes in the last pages of volume two of the *Diary* (346). While she leaves the question "unanswered" at that point, she does so before the volume closes, and in doing so summarizes the political theme of the work as well as indicating the progress of her odyssey from the inner to the outer. Before the war, she says, "I asserted through art the eternal against the temporal, I set up individual creativity against the decomposition of our historical world," referring both to her mode of writing and to its subject matter. With the world at war, she does not change her principles but broadens her scope.

> I had to make clear the relation of our individual dramas to the larger one, and our responsibility. . . . But the artist is not there to be at one with the world; he is there to transform it. He cannot belong to it, for then he would not achieve his task, which is to change. The struggle against destruction which I lived out in my intimate relationships had to be transposed and become of use to the whole world. (348-349)

---

[3] The episode provides an excellent example of the way Nin *uses* material from the *Diary* for the fiction. In *Four-Chambered Heart* it is the works of the realists that are burned deliberately in an opposite cause.

[4] Gunther Stuhlmann, "Preface" to volume two of the *Diary*, p. viii.

The Gonzalos believe in collective and violent action, the Nins in personal art that symbolically shadows forth the problems of the macrocosm. "Psychologically, a great personality is a circle touching something at every point. A circle with a core . . . widening until it joins the circle motions of the infinite" (249). The political activist is circumference only, a myopic Sisyphus.

iii

"This is Gulliver's country," writes Nin at the beginning of volume three of the *Diary* (12), and while it is at this point the Brobdingnagian aspects of America of which she is speaking, before the end of the volume she has come to recognize the features of the other three Swiftian countries in America as well. The theme of volume three is generally the contrast of cultures, specifically the Jamesian "international" theme. Like the other figures in her *Diary,* however, the Americans and Europeans are representative and it is the symbolical rather than the sociological aspects of the contrast that as usual concern her. "All around us there is excitement in place of exaltation, rush and action in place of depth, humor in place of feeling" (14); America, in short, represents the outside, the mirror of industry; Europe, the garden rooted in the culture of the past.

" 'Europe is decadent,' " says one of the innocents at home to Nin; " 'You must be happy to be in a healthy country' " (14). But as Nin realizes, what the American calls decadent is the European's courage to embrace all of life, and what he calls health is hygenic sterility. The European is the lusty lover of all life and death; the American seeks to "preserve" himself for himself: "They refuse to evolve, ripen, alter, out of fear of death. They try to cheat time by standing still and remaining virgin. They think one remains young by not living, not loving, not erring, not giving or spending or wasting one's self" (76).

The artist's desire to be independent, man's desire to make a new start, is natural and admirable, according to Nin. But the American has interpreted the impulse literally and practices it negatively. Like the anarchist, he wants absolutely to sever himself from the past and expends more effort in announcing his departure from than in perfecting it: "Here I feel a kind of shamefaced stealing from the European artists and a quick turnabout to deny any such influence" (120). And when she confronts one such American with his finger in the pie, he attempts to cover his mistake, like Gulliver and his sublimated attraction to the female Yahoo, by making her a special case: " 'You come from a sunken Atlantis.' (Again! How eager they are to imagine Europe sunken, and they able to create a new world!)" (42-43). But it is not simply that it is deceitful and a sign of prejudice that Nin objects to the American orphantilism, it is because it is self-destructive. " 'Can you imagine your future,' " she asks the literary Topsy, and when he admits he cannot, she explains: " 'Possibly because you are rejecting the past. The future takes its nourishment from the past and then converts it, produces a new alchemy. Feed on us before you bury us' " (42). It is not because she is a conservative but because she is an organicist that she objects to rootless art and hot-house blooms.

"New York is the very opposite of Paris" also in its lack of respect for humanity and in turn its unconcern for literature. "There is much talk about the 'world,' about millions, groups, but no warmth between human beings. They persecute subjectivity, which is a sense of inner life; an individual's concern with growth and self-development is frowned upon" (49). This ideological concern with the citizen rather than with the personality accounts for the two types of literature in America. First, the literature of social consciousness. In America it is not the literary or cultural value of a book that is prized but its sociological aspects, its realism, its topicality. "A book is judged almost entirely by a person's need, and what people respond to is either a reflection of themselves, a multiple mirror, or an elucidation of their time, a concern with their problems, fears, or a familiar atmosphere which is reassuring by its familiarity" (271). Such fiction, according to Nin, reveals and encourages the worst kind of narcissism and passivity; it is easier to photograph a scene than to paint it; the true "novel" requires attention, the newsreport can be comprehended in a glance. America they tell us is the richest and most undernourished country in the world; to Nin the literary scene reveals a similar paradox, quantity, but no quality. "Too much social consciousness, and not a bit of insight into human beings" (44).

As in her argument against American literary independence, it is more what the social critic cannot do than what he actually does that makes her speak out. Unlike the anarchist, when Nin is against something it is because of what she is *for*. And the specific problem here is that "When the artist is forced to enter the immediate present, he loses his own peculiar perspective which enables him to connect and relate past, present, and future" (51). Thus it is because she sees the artist's task as integrating humanity rather than as isolating a certain problem that she objects to extra-literary commitments. The artist's task is to influence "by contagion" (113) not by prescription. His task is to explore the city of the interior not "to meddle with political and practical constructions" (131). What is needed in America, then, is not the political novel but a better division of labor: "The old communities understood this. Each one had his role allotted to him. The poet to supply his visions, his song, his inspiration (from within) and the others to hunt, fish, build, and the wise men to interpret events, omens, the future" (113-114). To Nin, the artist should be provided for by society (93) and respected for his literary contribution.

Social-consciousness fiction is, then, the reflection and result of the mechanical rather than natural collective organization of America. The second type of American literature is symptomatic rather than indicative,

110

that is, it is the unhealthy consequence of an unnatural psychological condition. This is the literature of violence.

At the beginning of volume three Nin warns that America's "cult of toughness, its hatred of sensibility," its neglect of man's spiritual needs is creating a serious problem, "and someday it may have to pay a terrible price for this, because atrophy of feeling creates criminals" (28). The novel of violence fulfills the prophecy: "Each act of sex remains strangely unconsummated, a murder takes the place of it. What I see in this book, what cries behind windows, haunting every scene, sightless, voiceless, throughout the drama of violent acts, what is murdered each time anew, what passes from the one man to another, is a soul dispossessed by violence, crying to be born, *a soul not yet born*" (64). Although it is a specific work she is describing, the description applies to a good half of the works published in the recent decades, as Nin realizes: "But where is the whole vision which will catalyze this chaos and guide it to its birth? Is this the American nightmare: violence, castration, fragmentation?" (64-65). Nietzschean, Nin believes that destruction is part of creation, but American artists are trapped in destruction, because America decided to make Apollo its god; it is revenge that the modern writer is wreaking on his world, and behind it all is the suppressed but unconquerable Dionysus.

A final feature of America's rootlessness and the consequences it entails is the American woman. Two figures in particular represent the type to which Nin as a woman appears as the European contrast: one is "intellectual, but cold as a human being" (14), the masculine career woman; the other is the one who "gave her life to politics. She gave herself in a manner which gained the respect of the moralists, sociologists, missionaries, political party members. But my feeling was that she had run away from a confrontation with her self, from the task of training, nurturing, maturing it before giving it away" (225). The first type has sacrificed her feminine sensitivity for a masculine role; the second has forfeited a personal, intimate life for a public role. Both, in short belong to the realist camp, for their concern is with the external and superficial. In contrast, Nin reviews her struggles to be mother to two kinds of children, her own creations and those of others, To her, woman's initial problem is not to make herself heard but to hear herself, that is to understand what it is that needs expression. And from her own experience, what needs expression is the woman's feeling of vital connection not to the social scene but to the cosmos, "how to manifest the cosmic consciousness she feels" (241), how to perfect herself, not how to rival man (259). The true woman is anxious about a public role because it threatens a relationship to man that she wishes to maintain, that of lover and mother; she is by nature a "pisces," a giver, and her problem is how

111

to distribute her gifts, how to maintain her double role. And for this she needs "man's blessing and man's help" (234).[5]

It is against the atrophying social consciousness and the self-destructive violence of American life and literature that Nin slowly and quietly attempts to work: "I am far from blind, far from indifferent, but I will not indulge in impotent, passive despair. I will not add to the despair of the world. I am working on counterpoisons" (149). The first counterpoison is "cosmic consciousness" which "solves all dualities and divisions" (218), temporal and spatial, as well as racial and ideological. It is not an escape from reality but an escape from history, the nightmare of the Western world. The second positive measure is personal and ritualistic fiction: "Stories are the only enchantment possible, for when we begin to see our suffering as a story, we are saved. It is the balm of the primitive, the way to exorcise a terrifying life" (296). Nin, that is, does not believe in pseudo-primitivism— the external and superficial gestures of going native—but in the spiritual and imaginative return to the garden.

"When we are in conflict," writes Anaïs Nin retrospectively in the closing pages of volume three of the *Diary,* "we tend to make such sharp oppositions between ideas and attitudes, and get caught and entangled in what seems to be a hopeless choice" (299). As is usual, she uses herself as her best example, and as is also usual, her words extend into the general: "I opposed subjective to objective, imagination to realism. I thought that having gone so deeply into my own feelings and dramas I could never again reach objectivity and knowledge of others. But now I know that any experience carried out deeply to its ultimate leads you beyond yourself into a larger experience of others" (299). The comment provides an excellent indication of the progress of *Diary* three as well as of the unity of her world. For in her earliest public work she had advanced the same argument; "an experience, provided it is lived with intensity and sincerity, often leads out of itself into its opposite" (*Lawrence,* 107). Which means, not that her scope is limited, but the opposite, that it is archetypal: "It is always the same story one is telling. But from a different angle" (251).

iv

In volume four of the *Diary,* the main setting is Greenwich Village; the time, 1944–47, the last years of World War II and its aftermath. This is also the period when Nin's fictional work first begins to attract public attention, and thus in this volume the angle from which she continues the old story is the situation of the poet in a ruthlessly critical and fact-oriented climate. For her success in finding a publisher and an audience also means that the battles she fought in private—with Miller, with Gonzalo—must be pursued again in public—with literary critics and reviewers.

---

[5] For Nin's direct statement concerning the Women's Liberation Movement see "On Women's Liberation," *Under the Sign of Pisces,* II, no. 1 (Winter, 1971), pp. 1-4.

But she wages this war quietly. Neither by retaliation nor argument does she try to make critics see things her way. Such methods would be futile, since intuitive writing is by definition beyond rational demonstration and since her critics are those who have become too old or hardened to consider an alternative to their prescriptive perspectives. The "best attack," she tells a friend, "is to continue to work. To do better and better work, that is where to put my energy" (123), and to address her work and life style to those who have not surrendered their dreams for the security of the system—to those whom she calls "The Transparent Children" (101).

Her attraction to the young, she explains, arises from the similarity between the creative and the adolescent personality: "both live in a world of their own making. . . . Both the artist and the child create an inner world ruled by their fantasies or dreams. They do not understand the world of money, or the pursuit of power. They create without commercial intent. They rebel against existing conditions. They cannot be deceived. The realistic world for them is ruled by conscious compromises, self-betrayals, selling out" (99). There are two such types of children in volume four of the *Diary*.

"This quality, the quality of renewal, perpetual youthfulness, which I liked in the artist, I find in the homosexuals," Nin observes (188). For to her, the homosexual is seeking not physical pleasure but a relationship devoid of sex. Homosexual love is narcissistic; the other person is loved not for himself but as a projection of the self. The motivation behind such relationships, therefore, is not a perverted appetite but a desire to have unlimited possibilities to create for oneself "a joyous, facile, promiscuous world, natural, and without permanence" (126). It is these qualities, the childlike spontaneity and playfulness, that constitute the positive and attractive aspects of the homosexual.

There is, however, a great difference between the European and the American homosexual, according to Nin: "The Spanish homosexual or the French homosexual loved men but did not hate women" (126); the American homosexual is largely characterized by this hatred. The reasons for this, she suggests, are traumatic childhood experiences with females, in particular, and the puritanical caste of American culture, in general. In any case, "In the American homosexual it was the hatred of woman which was a perversity, for it distorted reality, and made expansion impossible" (126); in the American homosexual, the childlike quality becomes childishness, a refusal to grow up, motivated not by a creative desire to be mobile but by a fear of "totality, the absolute in love" (125). "There is a furtive quality to it all. Or else it comes out in irony, satire, or mockery of itself" (188).

The second type of children are the chronologically young, the adolescents and teenagers. As with the homosexuals, it is the gaiety and imaginative freedom of the young that appeal to Nin, though they too can be disappointing if they finally succumb to cultural pressures. For in America, to "grow up" means to become realistic; because of a confusion of strength and callousness, "The shell is America's most active contribution to the formation of character. A tough hide. Grow it early" (144).

Sensitivity must be either surrendered or persecuted; this is the dilemma facing the poet in the modern world. For this reason Nin sees the case of the mysterious Caspar Hauser as the prototype for the fate of "The Transparent Children" and employs the tale as the central motif of the fourth volume. According to her, "The story of Caspar Hauser is a story far more beautiful than that of Christ. It is the story of innocence, of a dreamer destroyed by the world. . . . Power, intrigue, evil cynicism join to murder him" (64).

Nin witnesses a symbolic reenactment of Caspar's destruction in the coming of age of a young man named Leonard W. This sensitive youth is brutalized by the world into its concept of a man: the soldier. Leonard, seventeen, comes to her by way of her book of short stories, *Under a Glass Bell*. After discovering that her mode of life is as honest and spontaneous as her manner of writing, he decides to leave his father—and his father's oil company—and to join her circle. Thus "the dream began" (46). In her company he feels free to "play" and to live his dreams. He reminds her of Caspar Hauser "because of his innocence and sudden insights. He has intuitions about people which are those of an old soul" (47). But then the dream sharply ends. Leonard is a man and the world is at war. The mature world dictates, " 'Go to war. Earn your living' " (82). It is not the demand that is wrong, Nin explains, but the implications and the consequences: "Accept our attitude toward life" is what the order means, and to obey this dictate involves laughing at one's earlier sensitivities as weaknesses. Thus when he writes to her from the army, it is "No more Caspar Hauser. That was a romantic concept of his vulnerability!" (91). When she sees him again, it is a "Leonard who had lost his dewiness, opalescence, transparence, by his life in the army. With rougher hands and skin, and now a lieutenant. A Leonard less shy, with a richer voice. He had chosen to go to Japan" (143).

In the literary world, Nin sees her own situation as a variation of the Caspar Hauser plot but herself as an undefeated Hauser. For as she explains ironically in an early letter to Leonard, Caspar died because he "was no poet . . . in the poet, the child, the adolescent, never dies" (74). She envisions being beaten by those who do not understand this, but she asserts that she will not be spiritually destroyed by them: "I will die a poet killed by the nonpoets, [but] will renounce no dream, resign myself to no ugliness, accept nothing of the world but the one I made myself" (177).

Two critics in particular represent the types of nonpoets who either deliberately or unwittingly are the enemies of the creative writer. Diana Trilling is representative of the literalist mentality. She assumes, observes Nin, that "because I had studied psychology I was writing case histories" (82). She also "complains that Lillian and her husband and children are unreal" (121) in *Ladders to Fire*. But Nin's very purpose, as she explains, is to create Lillian's sense of the unreality of her life: "How can one spend the length of a novel making something real which appears unreal to the central character?" (121). The problem, in short, is that the literalist is often incapable of recognizing and accepting psychological realism as a point of view. Such a critic demands of art a mirror image of the times.

Edmund Wilson typifies the academic mentality, antagonistic to the creative writer. A Cronus figure, he is also the type who hates " 'young writers. I hate them' " (88), but not because he is incapable of understanding their work or because he is insecure. It is because he is too settled and secure. The threat that such a critic presents is an indirect rather than a direct one: namely, authority and the tyranny of tradition. Unlike Trilling and the literalists, he does not become defensive and vindictive; he simply either ignores what he does not agree with, thereby damning it through indifference, or he makes prescriptions for work he likes in order to bring that work into line with the established *données* of literary craft. Wilson, for example, praises Nin's writing for its " 'amazing insights! Marvelous insights!' " but then explains that he " 'must be severe . . . *This Hunger* has no form. It is not concrete enough' " (83). He patronizes her by presenting her with a set of Jane Austen.

"Why does everyone here believe that by all of us thinking of nothing else but the mechanics of living, of history, we will solve all problems?" Nin asks toward the end of the fourth volume of her *Diary*. "Sometimes one has to be away to think properly" (190). Circumstances at this point literally force her to make such a desired withdrawal; the war is over and her status as a temporary resident can no longer be maintained. She must leave the United States and then reenter, if it is in America that she wishes to live. While she is considering the alternatives, she meets a young American from the West who, hearing that she is basing her decision upon her life in New York, wisely expostulates: "You mean that is all you know of America? New York is not America" (197).

Her journey to the South and West confirms the young man's words and her own faith in her ideals. The trip delivers her of "the toxics of New York" by introducing her to nature and to people "who were natural and gracious" and to "bigger artists, unconcerned with ambition" (222). Among the bigger artists, the two who figure in prominence are Lloyd Wright and Jean Varda. Wright, according to Nin, is "the poet of architecture. For him a building, a home, a stone, a roof, every inch of architecture has meaning, was formed from an inner concept" (210). Like her work, Wright's buildings are designed to "create a more beautiful and satisfying human environment" (211). Like hers, "his struggle is against uniformity and wholesale design," and he is continually opposed by the forces of commercialism: "The transient, the meretricious, the imitation, the pseudo rule the day" (212). In "Janko" Varda, the collage artist, Nin finds another ally, but of a rather different temperament. For him, "art is an expression of joy" (218); he is the poet who creates beauty from "scraps." Like the cultists of ugliness, he visits the junk heaps for his materials; unlike them, his purpose is to transform the ugly not to propagate it. Whereas they are motivated by a commitment to realism, he is inspired by a love of life and the magic of creation. To Nin, Varda is the only modern artist who creates fairy tales, "not the sickly-sweet tales of childhood but the sturdy fairy tale of the artist" (216).

When, as a result of her initial breakthrough as a writer, Nin is asked for a short autobiography, presumably for *Harper's Bazaar,* she replies with a letter which begins: "That was one question I was hoping you would not ask me but answer for me. . . . My real self is unknown. My work is merely an essence of this vast and deep adventure" (176). But later in the letter she does project an image of herself, and it is one which perfectly evokes the character of her writing as we have thus far come to know it: "I wrote, lived, loved like Don Quixote, and on the day of my death I will say: 'Excuse me, it was all a dream,' and by that time I may have found one who will say: 'Not at all, it was true, absolutely true' " (177).

In volume five of the *Diary* . . .

Bibliography

Works by ANAÏS NIN

Fiction:
(Children)   Children of the Albatross. New York: E. P. Dutton & Company, Inc., 1947.
(Heart)   Cities of the Interior. Vol. I. Denver: Alan Swallow, 1959. (Contains Ladders to Fire, Children of the Albatross, Four-Chambered Heart, A Spy in the House of Love, Solar Barque).
(Collages)   Collages. Denver: Alan Swallow, 1964.
              Four-Chambered Heart. New York: Duell, Sloan & Pearce, 1950.
(House)   House of Incest. New York: Gemor Press, 1959. (First published in Paris, 1936).
(Ladders)   Ladders to Fire. New York: E. P. Dutton & Company, Inc., 1946.
              "Le Merle Blanc," in The Booster (September, 1937), pp. 17-18.
              "The Paper Womb," in The Booster (December, 1937), pp. 3-5.
("Sabina")   "Sabina," in Chicago Review (Winter-Spring, 1962), pp. 45-60.
              "The Sealed Room," in Tiger's Eye, I (October, 1947), pp. 82-85.
(Seduction)   Seduction of the Minotaur. Denver: Alan Swallow, 1961.
              Solar Barque. Ann Arbor: Edwards Brothers, 1958.
              "Soundless Keyboard Orchestra," in Delta (Christmas, 1938), pp. 67-71.
(Spy)   A Spy in the House of Love. New York: British Book Centre, 1954.
              "The Synthetic Alchemist," in Two Cities: La Revue Bilingue de Paris (July 15, 1959), pp. 38-42.
              "The Trees Walk at Night," in Story, no. 139 (March-April, 1963), pp. 66-70.
(Bell)   Under a Glass Bell. New York: E. P. Dutton & Company, Inc., 1948 (first published New York, 1944).
(Winter)   Winter of Artifice. New York: Anaïs Nin Press, 1945. (First published in Paris, 1939).
Criticism: "Anaïs Nin on Hiram Haydn's Report from the Red Windmill," Voyages (Winter, 1970), pp. 29-30.
              "Anaïs Nin: Review of Rank's Art and Artist," Journal of the Otto Rank Association, III (December, 1968), pp. 94-97.
              "A Boost for Black Spring," The Booster (November, 1937), p. 27.
              "Comments on Neglected Books of the Past Twenty-five Years," in American Scholar (Spring, 1970), p. 337.
(Lawrence)   D. H. Lawrence: An Unprofessional Study. With an Introduction by Harry T. Moore. Chicago: The Swallow Press, Inc., 1964. (First published in Paris, 1932).
              "Marguerite Young: Woman of our time," Matrix: for she of the new aeon, I (Spring, 1970), pp. 13-14.

(Novel)   *The Novel of the Future.* New York and London: The Macmillan Company, 1968.

On Writing. New York: Gemor Press, 1947.

"The Poetic Novel—Bridge Between Inner and Outer Reality," *Journal of the Otto Rank Association,* VIII (June, 1970), pp. 25-30.

"Preface" to Henry Miller's *Tropic of Cancer.* New York: Grove Press, Inc., 1961, pp. xxi-xxxiii.

Realism and Reality. New York: Gemor Press, 1946.

"Woman in the Myth," *Twice a Year* (Fall-Winter, 1940; Spring-Summer, 1941).

"The Writer and the Symbols," *Two Cities* (April 15, 1959), pp. 33-40.

Diaries:

(I) *The Diary of Anaïs Nin: 1931-1934.* Edited and with an Introduction by Gunther Stuhlmann. New York: The Swallow Press and Harcourt Brace Jovanovich, Inc., 1966.

(II) *The Diary of Anaïs Nin: 1934-1939.* Edited and with a Preface by Gunther Stuhlmann. New York: The Swallow Press and Harcourt Brace Jovanovich, Inc., 1967.

(III) *The Diary of Anaïs Nin: 1939-1944.* Edited and with a Preface by Gunther Stuhlmann. New York: Harcourt Brace Jovanovich, Inc., 1969.

(IV) *The Diary of Anaïs Nin: 1944-1947.* Edited and with a Preface by Gunther Stuhlmann. New York: Harcourt Brace Jovanovich, Inc., 1971.

SECONDARY SOURCES

Books and Pamphlets:

Aldridge, John W., ed. *Critiques and Essays on Modern Fiction:* 1920-1951. New York: Ronald Press Company, 1952.

Booth, Wayne. *The Rhetoric of Fiction.* Chicago: University of Chicago Press, 1961.

Brodin, Pierre. *Présences Contemporaines: Écrivains Américains d'Aujourd'hui.* Paris: Nouvelles Éditions Debresse, 1964.

Brown, E. K. *Rhythm in the Novel.* Toronto: University of Toronto Press, 1950.

Brown, Norman O. *Life Against Death: The Psychoanalytic Meaning of History.* New York: Vintage Books, 1959.

————. *Love's Body.* New York: Vintage Books, 1966.

Cassirer, Ernst. *The Philosophy of Symbolic Forms.* Vol. II: "Mythical Thought." Translated by Ralph Manheim with an Introductory Note by Charles Hendel. New Haven and London: Yale University Press, 1968.

Dujardin, Edouard. *Les lauries sont coupés.* Introduction by Leon Edel. New York: New Directions, 1957.

Edel, Leon. *The Modern Psychological Novel.* New York: Grosset & Dunlap, 1964.

Eliade, Mircea. *Cosmos and History: The Myth of the Eternal Return.* Translated from the French by Willard R. Trask. New York: Harper & Row, 1959.

Ellmann, Richard and Charles Feidelson, Jr., eds. *The Modern Tradition: Backgrounds of Modern Literature.* New York: Oxford University Press, 1965.

Emerson, Ralph Waldo. *Selections from Ralph Waldo Emerson.* Edited by Stephen E. Whicher. Boston: Houghton-Mifflin Company, 1960.

Erikson, Erik H. *Childhood and Society.* Second Edition, Revised and Enlarged. New York: W. W. Norton & Company, Inc., 1963.

Evans, Oliver. *Anaïs Nin.* With a Preface by Harry T. Moore. Carbondale and Edwardsville: Southern Illinois University Press, 1968.

Fiedler, Leslie. *Love and Death in the American Novel.* New York: Criterion Books, 1960.

Fingarette, Herbert. *The Self in Transformation: Psychoanalysis, Philosophy & the Life of the Spirit.* New York: Basic Books, Inc., 1963.

Forster, E. M. *Aspects of the Novel.* London: Penguin Books, 1964.

Friedman, Melvin. *Stream of Consciousness: A Study in Literary Method.* New Haven: Yale University Press, 1955.

Hassan, Ihab. *Radical Innocence: Studies in the Contemporary American Novel.* New Jersey: Princeton University Press, 1961.

Holland, Norman N. *The Dynamics of Literary Response.* New York: Oxford University Press, 1968.

Isaacs, J. *An Assessment of Twentieth-Century Literature.* London: Secker and Warburg, 1951.

Jaeger, Werner. *Paideia: The Ideals of Greek Culture.* Vol. I: "Archaic Greece, The Mind of Athens." Translated from the German by Gilbert Highet. New York: Oxford University Press, 1965.

James, Henry. *The Future of the Novel: Essays on the Art of Fiction.* Edited with an Introduction by Leon Edel. New York: Vintage Books, 1956.

Johnstone, J. K. *The Bloomsbury Group.* New York: The Noonday Press, 1963.

Jung, C. G. *Psychology of the Unconscious.* Translated with an Introduction by Beatrice M. Hinkle. New York: Dodd, Mead and Company, 1957.

Lawrence, D. H. *Assorted Articles.* London: Martin Secker, 1930.

————. *Selected Literary Criticism.* Edited by Anthony Beal. New York: The Viking Press, 1956.

————. *Fantasia of the Unconscious.* London: William Heinemann Ltd., 1937.

————. *Psychoanalysis and the Unconscious.* New York: Thomas Seltzer, 1921.

————. *Studies in Classic American Literature.* London: Martin Secker, 1933.

Lesser, Simon O. *Fiction and the Unconscious.* With a Preface by Ernest Jones. New York: Vintage Books, 1957.

Lubbock, Percy. *The Craft of Fiction.* London: Jonathan Cape Ltd., 1924.

Miller, Henry. *Letters to Anaïs Nin.* Edited with an Introduction by Gunther Stuhlmann. New York: G. P. Putnam's Sons, 1965.

O'Connor, William Van, ed. *Forms of Modern Fiction.* Minneapolis: The University of Minnesota Press, 1948.

Perlès, Alfred. *My Friend Henry Miller.* London: Neville Spearman, 1955.

Phillips, William, ed. *Art and Psychoanalysis.* New York: Criterion Books, 1957.

Rank, Otto. *Art and Artist.* New York: Tudor Publishing Company, 1932.

————. *The Myth of the Birth of the Hero and Other Writings,* edited by Philip Freund. New York: Vintage Books, 1964.

Rogers, W. G. *Wise Men Fish Here*. New York: Harcourt Brace Jovanovich, Inc., 1965.

Stevick, Philip, ed. *The Theory of the Novel*. New York: The Free Press, 1967.

Van Ghent, Dorothy. *The English Novel: Form and Function*. New York, Evanston and London: Harper & Row, Publishers, 1961.

Widmer, Kingsley. *Henry Miller*. New York: Twayne Publishers, Inc., 1963.

Wilson, Edmund. *Axel's Castle*. New York: Charles Scribner's Sons, 1935.

Articles and Reviews:

Atlas, James. "The Diary of Anaïs Nin, v. III," *The Harvard Crimson* (December 4, 1969).

Balakian, Anna. "Review" of Oliver Evans' *Anaïs Nin, American Literature*, XLI (March, 1969), pp. 130–133.

————. "Sponge for the World's Tears," *Saturday Review* (July 22, 1967), pp. 38-39.

Baldanza, Frank. Review of Anaïs Nin's Writings. *Minnesota Review*, II (Winter, 1962), pp. 263-271.

Barron, David B. "A Study in Symbolism," *Psychoanalytic Review*, XXXIV, (1947), pp. 395-431.

Becker, George J. "Realism: An Essay in Definition," *Modern Language Quarterly*, XX (1949), pp. 184-197.

Bradbury, Malcolm. Review of *Seduction of the Minotaur*. *Punch* (June 21, 1961), pp. 953-954.

————. Review of *Under a Glass Bell*. *Guardian* (September 12, 1968), p. 14.

Buckmaster, Henrietta. Review of *The Diary of Anaïs Nin: 1931-1934*. *Christian Science Monitor* (June 16, 1966), p. 5.

Burford, William. "The Art of Anaïs Nin," in *On Writing*. New York: Gemor Press, 1947, pp. 5-14.

Casey, Florence. Review of *The Novel of the Future*. *Christian Science Monitor* (January 14, 1969), p. C1.

"Children of the Albatross," *New Yorker* (November 8, 1960), p. 122.

"Cities of the Interior," in *Two Cities* (May 15, 1960), pp. 100-103.

"The Computer and the Poet," *Saturday Review* (July 23, 1966), p. 42.

Davis, Robert Gorham. "Anaïs Nin's 'Children of Light and Movement'," *New York Times Book Review* (November 23, 1947), p. 36.

————. "The Fantastic World of Anaïs Nin," *New York Times Book Review* (March 28, 1948), p. 24.

Delacroix, Jean-Jacques. "Un Roman Passione: Le Journal D'Anaïs Nin," *Elle* (22 Juin, 1970), pp. 58-61.

"D. H. Lawrence." New Yorker (May 30, 1964), p. 36.

Edel, Leon. "Journals," *Times Literary Supplement* (July 21, 1966), p. 633.

————. "Life Without Father," *Saturday Review* (May 7, 1966), p. 91.

"Editorial," in *The Booster* (September, 1937), p. 5.

Edmiston, Susan. "Portrait of Anaïs Nin," *Mademoiselle* (October, 1970), pp. 134–135, 222–225.

Evans, Oliver. "Anaïs Nin and the Discovery of Inner Space," *Prairie Schooner*, XXXVI (1962), 217-231.

Fanchette, Jean. "Notes Pour Une Préface," in *Two Cities* (April 15, 1959), pp. 56-60.

Fichter, Robert. "Anaïs Nin Recalled," *Boston Sunday Traveler, Book Guide* (January 4, 1970), pp. 6-7.

Foster, Richard. "Criticism as Rage," *A D. H. Lawrence Miscellany*, Harry T. Moore ed. Carbondale: Southern Illinois University Press, 1959, pp. 312-325.

Frank, Joseph. "Spatial Form in Modern Literature," *Sewanee Review*, LIII (1945), Part I, 221-240; Part II, 432-456; Part III, 643-653.

Friedman, Melvin J. "Andre Malraux and Anaïs Nin," *Contemporary Literature*, II (Winter, 1970), pp. 104-113.

Fuller, John. Review of *Four-Chambered Heart*. *New Statesman* (May 1, 1964), p. 688.

Fulop-Miller, René. "Freudian Noah's Ark," *New York Times Book Review* (January 29, 1950), p. 4.

Garrigue, Jean. Review of *The Diary of Anaïs Nin: 1931-1934*. *New York Times Book Review* (April 24, 1966), p. 1.

——————. Review of *The Diary of Anaïs Nin: 1939–1944*. *New York Times Book Review* (November 23, 1969), p. 28.

Geismar, Maxwell. "Temperament vs. Conscience," *Nation* (July 24, 1954), pp. 75-76.

Glicksberg, Charles I. "The Psychology of Surrealism," *Polemic*, VIII (1947), pp. 46-55.

Goyen, William. "Bits and Images of Life," *New York Times Book Review* (November 29, 1964), p. 5 and p. 24.

Graham, K. Review of *Under a Glass Bell*. *Listener* (September 5, 1968), p. 313.

Hahn, Emily. "*Winter of Artifice*, by Anaïs Nin," *T'ien Hsia Monthly*, IX (November, 1939), pp. 435-438.

Hardwick, Elizabeth. "Fiction Chronicle," *Partisan Review*, XV (June, 1948), pp. 705-708.

Hauser, Marianne. "Thoughts on *The Diary of Anaïs Nin*," *Journal of the Otto Rank Association*, VIII (June, 1970), pp. 61-67.

Hicks, Granville. Review of *The Novel of the Future*. *Saturday Review* (January 25, 1969), p. 26.

Jameson, Storm. "The Writer in Contemporary Society," *The American Scholar* (Winter, 1965-66), pp. 67-77.

Kirsch, Robert. "Studying Masterwork of Noted Writer Anaïs Nin," *Los Angeles Times* (November 29, 1969), p. 64.

Lyons, Herbert. "Surrealist Soap Opera," *New York Times Book Review* (October 20, 1946), p. 16.

McEvilly, Wayne. "Two Faces of Death in Anaïs Nin's *Seduction of the Minotaur*," *New Mexico Quarterly* (Winter-Spring, 1969), pp. 179-192.

McLaughlin, Richard. "Shadow Dance," *Saturday Review* (December 20, 1947), p. 16.

MacNamara, Desmond. "Nin et Al," *New Statesman* (December 1, 1967), pp. 778-779.

Maloff, Saul. "The Seven Veils," *Newsweek* (July 3, 1967), p. 76.

Marcus, Steven. "The Novel Again," *Partisan Review*, XXIX (1962), pp. 159-195.

Mazzocco, Robert. "To Tell You the Truth," *New York Review of Books* (September 8, 1966), pp. 6-8.

Meras, Phyllis. *Book World* (November 30, 1969), p. 16.

Metzger, Deena. "Insight, Intuition, Dreams. . . ," *Los Angeles Free Press* (January 30, 1970), p. 34. See also earlier reviews (April 29, 1966), (July 28, 1967).

Miller, Henry. "Of Art and the Future," in *Sunday After the War*. New York: New Directions, 1944, pp. 146-160.

—————. "Letter to Anaïs Nin regarding one of her books," in his *Sunday After the War*. New York: New Directions, 1944, pp. 284-297.

—————. "More about Anaïs Nin," in his *Sunday After the War*. New York: New Directions, 1944, pp. 276-284.

—————. "Un Etre Étoilique," in his *The Cosmological Eye*. New York: New Directions, 1939, pp. 269-291.

Morris, Lloyd. "Anaïs Nin's Special Art," *New York Herald Tribune Book Review* (March 12, 1950), p. 17.

Morse, J. Mitchell. "The Choreography of 'The New Novel'," *Hudson Review* XVI (1963), 64.

Mudrick, Marvin. "Humanity is the Principle," *Hudson Review*, VII (1954-55), 612-614.

Nyren, Dorothy, ed. "Anaïs Nin," in *A Library of Literary Criticism*, Second Edition. New York: Fredrick Ungar Publishing Co., 1961, pp. 356-358.

Perlès, Alfred. "Fathers, Daughters and Lovers," *Purpose*, XII (January-March, 1940), pp. 45-48.

Pochoda, Elizabeth. "Books," (Review of the *Diaries*). *Glamour* (March, 1970), p. 66.

Rolo, Charles J. "The Very Special World of Anaïs Nin," *Atlantic* (February, 1950), p. 86.

Rosenfeld, Paul. "Refinements of a Journal," *Nation* (September 26, 1942), pp. 276-277.

Rosenfeld, Isaac. "Psychoanalysis as Literature," *New Republic* (December 17, 1945), pp. 844-845.

Sayre, Nora. Review of *The Diary of Anaïs Nin: 1931-1934. New Statesman* (September 16, 1966), p. 402.

Schlesinger, Marian C. "Anaïs Nin: an era recalled," *Boston Globe* (December, 1969).

Schneider, Duane. "The Art of Anaïs Nin," *The Southern Review*, VI (Spring, 1970), pp. 506-514.

Shapiro, Karl. "The Charmed Circle of Anaïs Nin," *Book Week* (May 1, 1966), p. 3.

—————. "Is Poetry an American Art?", *College English*, XXV (March, 1964), pp. 395-405.

Smith, Harrison. "Ladies in Turmoil," *Saturday Review* (November 30, 1946), p. 13.

Stern, Daniel. "Princess of the Underground," *Nation* (March 4, 1968), pp. 311-315.

Tindall, Gillian. "Doldrums," *New Statesman* (September 6, 1968), p. 292.

Trilling, Diana. "Fiction in Review," *Nation* (January 26, 1946), pp. 105-107.

Under The Sign of Pisces: Anaïs Nin and Her Circle. (The Nin Newsletter edited by Richard Centing and Benjamin Franklin, V).

Williams, William Carols. "Men. . . Have No Tenderness," *New Directions* (1942), pp. 429-436.

Wilson, Edmund. "Books," *New Yorker* (November 16, 1946), p. 130.

————. "Review of 'This Hunger'," *New Yorker* (November 10, 1945), pp. 73-74.

"Woman of Words: *The Journals of Anaïs Nin,*" *Times Literary Supplement* (June 11, 1970), p. 633.

Young, Marguerite. "Marguerite Young on Anaïs Nin," *Voyages* (Fall, 1967).

Young, Vernon. "Five Novels, Three Sexes, and Death," *Hudson Review*, I, no. 3, pp. 427-429.

Zinnes, Harriet. "Anaïs Nin's Work Reissued," *Books Abroad*, XXXVII (1963), pp. 283-286.

————. "No Mystery Lost," *American Scholar*, XXXVI (Winter, 1966-67), 150-154.

Index

125

127